About Island Press

Island Press is the only nonprofit organization in the United States whose principal purpose is the publication of books on environmental issues and natural resource management. We provide solutions-oriented information to professionals, public officials, business and community leaders, and concerned citizens who are shaping responses to environmental problems.

In 2006, Island Press celebrates its twenty-second anniversary as the leading provider of timely and practical books that take a multidisciplinary approach to critical environmental concerns. Our growing list of titles reflects our commitment to bringing the best of an expanding body of literature to the environmental community throughout North America and the world.

Support for Island Press is provided by the Agua Fund, The Geraldine R. Dodge Foundation, Doris Duke Charitable Foundation, The William and Flora Hewlett Foundation, Kendeda Sustainability Fund of the Tides Foundation, Forrest C. Lattner Foundation, The Henry Luce Foundation, The John D. and Catherine T. MacArthur Foundation, The Marisla Foundation, The Andrew W. Mellon Foundation, Gordon and Betty Moore Foundation, The Curtis and Edith Munson Foundation, Oak Foundation, The Overbrook Foundation, The David and Lucile Packard Foundation, The Winslow Foundation, and other generous donors.

The opinions expressed in this book are those of the author(s) and do not necessarily reflect the views of these foundations.

Ritual House

Ritual House

Drawing on Nature's Rhythms for Architecture and Urban Design

RALPH L. KNOWLES

● ISLANDPRESS *Washington · Covelo · London*

ISLAND PRESS is a trademark of The Center for Resource Economics.

Library of Congress Cataloging-in-Publication data.
Knowles, Ralph L.

Ritual house : drawing on nature's rhythms for architecture and urban design /
Ralph Knowles.— 1st ed.
p. cm.
Includes bibliographical references and index.
ISBN 1-59726-050-9 (cloth : alk. paper)
ISBN 1-59726-051-7 (pbk. : alk. paper)
1. Architecture—Human factors. 2. Architecture—Environmental aspects.
3. Architecture and solar radiation. 4. Solar energy. 5. City planning. I. Title.
NA2542.4.K66 2006
720'.47—dc22   2005020629

British Cataloguing-in-Publication data available.

Printed on recycled, acid-free paper

Design by David Bullen Design

Manufactured in the United States of America
10 9 8 7 6 5 4 3 2 1

To MER

Contents

Foreword

From his early writings about solar geometry—the physics of sun and earth—Ralph Knowles has become increasingly interested in the cultural response, the rituals and built artifacts that respond to the sun. It is not only the trace of the shadow cast, it is the flux of life that responds, whether the movement of the Anasazi Indians in and around the pueblos to take advantage of daily and seasonal sun or activities of modern living. Life on earth follows the sun as it arches across our skies in predictable ways. Knowles' early books were about that geometry. The range of human responses is richer, more unpredictable, and inspiring. This book is about that poetry.

Although this book is about the sun, buildings, and cities, Knowles has not given us a text about solar design. Look to earlier books for those texts. This book is based on astute observation and reflection, and is thus far wiser. It relates incidents and anecdotes, and is thus more interesting.

I recall a lecture that Ralph Knowles gave before an audience of architecture students, faculty, and professionals. He was showing illustrations of Acoma Pueblo and his studies that indicated solar angles that could possibly explain what was in the mind of the builders of these ancient cities. Knowles stood in front of the lecture podium, deliberately placing his feet and facing the hall. He asked us to imagine that he was facing south at the center of a sundial or solar clock. With arms raised and pointing in opposite directions to left and right (due east and west), he said that on two days of the year, the vernal and autumnal equinoxes, "the sun rises here [waving his left hand] and sets here [waving the right hand], no matter where we are standing at any position in the northern hemisphere." He then stretched his arms back and explained that, depending on our exact latitude, this might be where the sun rises and sets in summer and then moving his arms forward, where it might rise and set in winter. He then explained how the altitude of the sun depends on latitude, tracing the arc of the sun with his arms as we might see it in winter (low in the sky) and in summer (high in the sky).

The lecture was in an auditorium with fixed seating. But more than half of the audience was placing their arms and hands in similar positions, as everyone relaxed, laughed, and at the same time, became familiar with the elemental lessons of solar geometry. They were finally able to "get it." A complex topic was made easy to visualize and to internalize as part our own physical awareness. With this introduction, Knowles went through a series of studies of sun angles and architecture, always relating it back to the first elemental exercise of seasonal and daily sun position that we were able to understand.

This is an example of the lucid and elegant way that Ralph Knowles has made generations of architectural students and practitioners aware of the secrets of the sun. He has helped us understand how solar geometry can make designs of our buildings and cities climate responsive, open to the sun when it is beneficial for people and plants and shaded when the sun is an unwelcome burden.

Ralph Knowles has made this contribution in a lifetime of research, writing and teaching. His method of teaching has been based principally in the design studio, where interaction with students and with the subject matter at hand is primary. In teaching architectural students about solar geometry, he devised a heliodon or "sun machine," essentially a lamp by which one can easily retrace and model the daily and seasonal passage of the sun. With this, he posed challenges for students: to design arrangements of buildings so that they shared equally in winter sun, or in another assignment, to design a building form and shading devices so that is exposed entirely to winter sun but shaded entirely in summer (no easy trick). Among the most challenging of the assignments was to ask students to design a series of increasingly dense housing arrangements such as one would find in a city like Los Angeles, applying "sun-rights" zoning (providing for equal sun exposure for all building sites). The students then were asked to calculate whether the number of units with equal sun rights would be higher or lower than what is currently permitted without sun rights zoning. The answer—of great significance in any city in the United States or elsewhere—is that applying sun-rights zoning does not restrict or limit the number of housing units on a site. The studies demonstrate that with sun-rights zoning an equal (and in some cases, increased) number of units could be placed on a site as allowed by current zoning, with the added benefit that every unit had equal access to winter sun. Without quite realizing it, the students who participated in the design studies taught by Knowles were also undertaking significant research, utilizing design to test the limits of a hypothesis (in this case concerning zoning and land-use formulations, policies, and laws).

As a career-long interest for over fifty years, Ralph Knowles has developed such studies of the sun and its implications for architecture and urban design. He was engaged in these studies and published his first books well before the 1970s OPEC oil embargo brought energy efficient design to the fore. His books became part of the required reading lists in architectural schools and professional practices devoted to energy and architecture. From this prodigal beginning, his studies have grown in breadth and depth—each layer of understanding has led to and revealed yet another level of understanding and insight. This book is testament and record of this understanding that results from a lifetime of study, reflection and inspiration.

This book is a great read on profoundly felt and clearly communicated ideas of life in society and on this planet. The writing carries the author's own voice—conversational, entertaining, and to the point. It is thus heart felt. It is understandable. The writing is precise, that is, the words are carefully crafted, but always reaching beyond to larger interpretation, expanding one's thought. Is that not the goal of all literature?

The subject is mundane, in the sense of "of this world" and apparent, but written so that the slightest detail of the observed environment is rendered inspirational and poetic. The reader is lead from appearance to deep and satisfying stories, metaphors that convey understanding of the author's unique view of architecture and the world.

Ralph Knowles's writing asks us to pay attention to detail, found by observation of the sun's traces across a patio or plaza, and the response of leaf, flower, bird, animal, and humans to the gift of the sunrise and sunset. We may be attracted first to the grace of a particular detail, be it a flowering plant or tree, but then we are doubly rewarded when we look at it longer and study the logic of its making. With reflection and time, this can convey lessons larger than itself, connecting us to the beauty and wisdom of all of nature. A close reading of this book is equally rewarding.

Donald Watson

Preface

 This book focuses on the maintenance of comfort and joy in our buildings through policies and designs that reconnect our lives to the rhythms of nature. It addresses the entire design community, including architects, planners, and landscape and interior designers. It is written, though, to be available to a general audience. No specialized knowledge is required for its understanding.

 It addresses one of the gravest problems of our day: the lack of commitment to a sustainable relationship between human beings and the natural environment. Clearly not a new concern, it is one that has become critically multiplied by unprecedented, worldwide energy usage and urbanization.

 I was reminded of the problem on a family trip to Phoenix, Arizona, some years ago. As we moved closer to the city, we saw from the highway a field of identical mobile housing units, each with a latticed air conditioner on its rooftop. Our youngest daughter, then barely big enough to see out the back window, quietly watched as we passed the scene. Then, no doubt with the upcoming Christmas holidays in mind, she asked in a worried voice, "How will Santa Claus get down the chimneys?"

This landscape of sealed isolation and our daughter's anxious response to it provide a background for this book, reminders of two parts of the same problem. The first and more universal part of the problem, the devastating environmental effects of our reliance on fossil fuels, has been thoroughly treated by others and therefore has, in this book, not been given an in-depth treatment. Rather, it is the second and more personal part of the problem, a disconnect between our private, domestic lives and the rest of nature, that has been given the most serious and careful thought.

In the course of examining our individual detachment from nature, the book explores the historical importance of sheltering methods that once linked people practically and spiritually to their environments. We have largely abandoned such modes when high-energy systems can automatically adjust our buildings to weather and climate. And yet a close examination of older traditions shows that patterns of social behavior, rituals that followed nature's complex rhythms, have been a time-honored condition of ecological balance, of personal choice, and of creativity. Consequently, this work posits the notion that these objectives can be reached by engaging rhythmic nature more closely than we now do. We can make shelters that actively enhance our participation in places, encouraging responses to climate that, through repetition, evolve into personal rituals, linking us to a place, adding meaning to our lives.

The book is organized in three major parts. The first part is more descriptive than analytical, concerned with people's feelings more than with precise measurements. It opens with actual accounts of traditional sheltering rituals gathered from around the world. Some of these have derived from *migration:* people moving long distances across great landscapes or merely across a room. Others have issued from *transformation:* changes of space resulting from repeatedly opening and closing a window, a shutter, a tent flap, or a courtyard cover. Finally, many have their roots in *metabolism:* crowding together to share body heat or gathering close to a warming fire. Regardless of their basis, the accounts all tell of a ritual connection between nature's rhythms and sheltering actions that enliven people's thoughts and free their creative imaginations.

The book then addresses issues of extraordinary urban growth, the way unprecedented changes of setting have altered the rhythms and rituals of our lives. First, a history of growth is traced in northeastern Ohio that typifies the changes in American life from wilderness to town over the past 200 years. The setting then shifts to Los Angeles, an urban region that exemplifies the ways our dependence on mechanical–electrical systems for comfort is progressively alienating us from nature. Since a majority of the world's population is expected to occupy large cities by 2030, the quality of life for most people will soon depend on the quality of urban living.

Finally, the book proposes and describes a practical tool that professionals can use to instruct urban growth for a better connection to nature for energy, comfort, and choice. It presents new studies of the *solar envelope,* the author's internationally recognized zoning device for solar access in cities. The solar envelope provides architects and urban designers with a design analysis tool by which to understand and implement solar access to buildings for passive solar heating, solar control, and daylighting as well as for active systems. It provides for low-impact development and opens new aesthetic possibilities for both designer and dweller. Additionally, this research explores the *interstitium,* a dynamic component of the solar envelope that advances the integration of traditional methods of adaptation to climate. These studies support the dynamism of a new design paradigm, one based on a dialogue with nature that encourages the ritual use of space and will give this new architecture its identity.

Acknowledgments

I would like to acknowledge the advice and assistance of the following people. First and foremost is the invaluable help of my wife, Mary. For months, we often sat side by side at the computer where she was the first to read and to help correct the text for clarity of language and for the appropriateness and order of topics. She also drew on her background in geography to help create critical linkages between different parts of the book. Next, I'm indebted to particular members of the USC School of Architecture: Richard Berry for his early work on the solar envelope; Karen Kensek whose computer generations first helped visualize the interstitium; Pierre Koenig who collaborated on the wind studies of courtyards; and Doug Noble for his continuing support and helpful conversations. Students of the USC School of Architecture have been recognized by name in the text along with their very important contributions to this work; my sincerest apologizes to those many whose names are not listed under images of large collective projects. I also want to thank the scattered friends and past students who, through the Internet, have helped to provide an intercultural aspect of the book. Finally, my sincerest thanks to all those at Island Press who worked so diligently to bring this book to publication.

Ritual House

1 | Sheltering

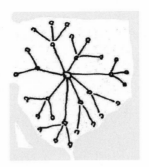

W<small>E HUMAN BEINGS, IN ALL PARTS OF THE WORLD AND</small> in all types of society, seek shelter—a building, a tent, or some other structure that keeps us safe and comfortable. We look for protection from the physical threats of nature and each other, a ceaseless quest that has produced an impressive array of forms. Besides protecting our bodies, we also seek a haven for our souls, our minds, and our spirits. We search for the joys of a home as well as the refuge of a house. In this less tangible regard, the static concept of a *shelter* gives way to the dynamic concept of *sheltering*.

As we occupy dwellings, we make certain adjustments for comfort in response to changes in the natural environment. We repeat these adjustments in concert with the unique rhythms of weather and climate in our particular setting. This repetition can give rise to rituals that feed our souls.

These ritual acts of sheltering help explain who we are and where we are in the world. Their development can range from the spiritual to the material, from the hidden to the obvious, from the personal to the communal. Whatever the case, ritual imparts meaning to the ebb and flow of a place.

This book explores the creative potential of such rituals by comparing modes of sheltering from traditional to modern, in places from rural to urban. It then proposes a design paradigm that, by reconnecting our lives to the rhythms of nature, encourages the ritual use of space as a way to conserve energy and to enhance the quality of life.

Making and Keeping

In the modern world we are abandoning traditional ways of sheltering. People everywhere are leaving farms and villages to live in towns and cities, and ancient forms of sheltering are being forgotten. Still, even in a mechanized world, all things must finally respond to nature. Long-established traditions offer a valuable model for today.

When most people depended directly on the land and lived close to nature, their modes of sheltering reflected centuries of learning how to live in a place. Dwellings were well adapted, sited, and shaped in response to local conditions of weather and climate. Corresponding patterns of behavior evolved through generations to match the cycles of time. Spring planting was carried out against a backdrop of fresh green leaves and flowering branches; harvest, against deep colors and bright fruit. Each season was separately ordered like an ancient stringed instrument, a kithara or a lyre, with its own unique resonator. Then cycles repeated as each year brought forth the same rhythmic responses. Rituals belonged to a natural world.

We, in the modern world, identify with growth, making new things in new places. Partly this is the consequence of a universal need to rapidly house people moving from rural to urban settings. Partly it is the result of a swelling global economy that rewards ever-expanding markets over constancy, development over a steady state, and novelty over tradition. The modern background of our lives has a strong sense of linearity and progress, an "arrow of time" replacing traditional cycles. Now, our sheltering rituals seldom mirror the rhythms of nature.

Our predilection for growth raises doubts about a sustainable future. Developers do not pay the utility bills for heating and cooling, lighting and ventilating our buildings. Consequently, designers are encouraged to install energy-intensive systems, "machines for living" that override natural variation. Dwellers who do pay the monthly bills are not always aware of the accumulating costs because they pay in countless small amounts over time, not in a more painful lump sum. Nor do many realize that over one-third of all the energy they consume each year in the United States goes for keeping their buildings comfortable. Over the 50- to 100-year average lifetime of these buildings, the energy price is staggering. In the simplest terms, we "build cheap" and "maintain expensive."

Additionally, and more to the point of this book, we have lost a challenge to our imaginations. Modern buildings automatically reduce natural variation to a narrow range of light, heat, and humidity without our direct involvement. We have gained uniform standards of comfort, but we have lost the sense of harmony that derives from experiencing the complex rhythms of nature. When we flatten and simplify nature, we lessen the need for many customarily repeated acts that open choices for self-expression.

I don't mean to suggest that we are somehow ennobled by a wholesale return to more primitive levels of adaptation. There is real suffering in being too hot or too cold, or in having to migrate immense distances to follow the seasons. The permanent places where we spend time do need to reduce stress on our minds and bodies. But there is a real question of means: do our buildings have to hide from us every small variation in the environment that might repeatedly summon us to action?

Rather, something deeply reassuring comes when our actions are consonant with the motions of nature. It is a reaffirmation of our own existence—a continuous call for choices that define who we are as individuals. Our need for this call should not be underestimated nor trivialized by design.

My challenge to designers is to acknowledge and celebrate the rhythmic nature of nature. All things respond to change and to transitions from one state of the environment to another: hot to cold, wet to dry, calm to breezy. Some of these changes are random, as when a passing cloud releases a brief shower, cooling a hot day. Others, though, recur at predictable intervals. We can expect

Morning and Evening on the Scottish Isle of Skye.

the sun to rise and set, the spring to follow winter, and the rains to come in their season. By working in sympathy with the rhythms of nature, architects and planners can help meet the needs of future generations. They can, as well, cause profound changes in the way people identify with their environments.

Rhythm

Cycle and epicycle, the face of the entire world is changed in rhythmic patterns. We may remain still and watch as natural alternations of time transform a landscape. Or we may join directly in the customary actions of people as they go from place to place over hours or seasons. Whether we stand and watch, or move with the ebb and flow, there is an impression of recurring boundaries in space. This is happening all the time and is the thing that really matters.

Landscapes are fixed only momentarily. A passing day on the Scottish Isle of Skye transforms the scene. Early morning mist grays the distant hills and softens the outline of a lighthouse across Loch na Dal. Shrubbery in the foreground blends with the shady

face of the house, both revealed only in dark silhouette. Only the roof of the house is highlighted, sketched in by a brighter edge of dormers. A cool breeze ruffles the loch.

In contrast, sunset draws attention to the distant lighthouse across the now dark water. The wind has changed direction and is warmer. The pale clouds of morning are by now grayed in the twilight. Foreground bushes independently catch the light. A small window, almost invisible in the morning, takes over one bright wall of the house. The rock wall shines while the roof recedes in shadow. And seasons will spread over it all.

RHYTHMIC BOUNDARIES IN SPACE

Spatial boundaries in the natural world have their own rhythmic character. For example, in the Owens Valley of California, where a 30-year precipitation cycle has been observed, separate plant communities advance and retreat. Yellow pine advances during wet years while chaparral advances during dry ones. The result is a region of mixing, a "tension zone" between the two plant communities where natural conditions are in constant flux.

Rhythmic boundaries can be seen in nature at all scales. Almost everyone can recall seeing ice crystals in the shadows of a rock. On a winter night tiny spikes appear everywhere. Then in the morning, the sun begins to melt all but those spikes hidden in the rock's shadow. As the sun moves from east to west, the shadow shifts and, by sunset, only a frosty crescent remains just to the north of the rock. Then it is night and the whole cycle starts over again.

The rhythms of natural boundaries are often complex and contrapuntal. This is evident at the beach where we can see a combination of different rhythms in the rising and falling of the ocean's surface. Waves act at the fastest tempo chasing birds, children, and barking dogs a few feet up the sand, then tempting them back again. If we stay for most of a day, we can watch the tide ebb and flow, shifting the stage from lower to higher on the beach. If we return on successive days over the course of a month, we will see the effect of a lunar cycle on the life in this tidal zone. And finally, if we return at different seasons of the year, our impressions will swing gradually to and fro as, within the single harmonic texture, each different rhythm retains its separate character.

Just as in nature, rhythmic boundaries also define the spaces we ourselves make and occupy. Most people understand architectural space as enclosed by fixed elements such as floors, ceilings, and walls. Yet space can be thought of dynamically as well, defined by passing sensations of sound, smell, and shadow.

Shadows from a wall alternately expand and contract. And, although we tend to see shadows only as a darker portion of a lighter plane, in fact they have volume, a space we can occupy for a while. How long we might be able to stay within a shadow can depend on the wall's orientation to the sun. Think of a garden wall in two orientations with a gateway through it.

A wall facing east and west will emphasize a daily rhythm. Morning sun strikes the east side, casting a shadow to the west. As the sun advances, the shadow shrinks, nearly disappearing by noon. Then as afternoon sun strikes the west side, a shadow grows on the east, reversing the picture. Anybody seeking sunshine must move daily from east to west through the gate in the wall. Seeking shade, they will pass in the opposite direction.

By comparison, a wall facing north and south will accentuate a seasonal rhythm. Summer shadows at midday will be small, having shrunk through the spring to a thin ribbon at the base of the north side. Winter shadows will grow northward during the fall before cycling back toward the wall throughout the spring. Clearly there is a problem with finding a cool shady place to sit in summer; and if the wall overshadows our garden in winter, there may be a problem finding a warm sunny place as well.

Rhythmic boundaries of space emerge depending on which of our senses we are using. Is it by light or heat that we appreciate a moving shadow? Is it by busy daytime sounds through an open window that we are first made aware of a street, then released from its hold as evening sounds subside? Is it by delicious smells of morning coffee filling the air that a kitchen ebbs and flows daily into the rest of the house? Space thus defined does not have fixed dimensions of distance, area, or volume. Instead, passing sensations rhythmically alter the proportions of space.

DOMAINS OF CHOICE IN TIME

The anthropologist Gregory Bateson observed that a real choice depends on comparing at least two different *somethings*; one something won't do.[1] But if we are to be sure that the possibilities are genuine, they must exist reasonably close to each other in our experience. Spatially, a choice exists between different sensations. Rhythm helps in this regard by alternating our experience of things, one after another, for easy comparison. Of course, the tempo of change must be neither too fast nor too slow. We must be able to *experience* the difference for it to *make* a difference.

Morning and Afternoon Shadows: Cast by an east–west-facing wall. (North to the left.)

Summer and Winter Shadows: Cast by a north–south-facing wall. (North to the right.)

A sheltering choice appears at the boundary where space is temporarily divided: to occupy a warm space or a cool one, wet or dry, light or dark. The choice can be conceived based on real sensations where a person can actually feel the difference. Or the choice can rest on the belief that a difference will soon appear. A choice based on natural rhythms will always return over time.

While rhythmic experiences may drive us to choose, they do not determine how we will act. Individuals and even whole cultures may respond quite differently. One person may move toward the comforting sounds and smells of the kitchen, another may move away from the distractions. The Canadian may desire sunshine while in the same setting the Mexican prefers shade. Yet, common to all is the temporal circumstance of making a choice.

Refuge

Shelter is usually understood as object, a building or a cave . . . something that protects us. Architecture is often spoken of as composition, "frozen music" that affixes one thing against another. But the people who seek refuge are not frozen or fixed in time. Their relationship to these shelters is a dynamic one.

Sheltering is the concept that recognizes this dynamic relationship, the ways our bodies and emotions respond to different measures of time. When we live in a place, we modify it for comfort, choice, and a sense of well-being. Sheltering, therefore, is not simply about a building but about a course of repeated actions in relation to the building.

To the extent that we are a natural process, we must expect our own acts of sheltering to follow nature. Three basic adaptive modes of the natural world apply to us as well: *migration, transformation,* and *metabolism.* Of these three methods, only metabolism in its modern, mechanical form fails to change the boundaries of space rhythmically. Instead, it often works from a premise of uniform conditioning of space. The resulting sensory monotone produces a dilemma, not a true choice: we can only select that space or none at all.

MIGRATION

The adaptive migrations of people follow the rhythms of nature. Some movements retrace ancient pathways for miles over periods of weeks. Others track hardly any distance at all through different rooms of a house. Regardless of distance, migrations tend to follow days and seasons.

It may be argued that moving about for comfort does not really change the boundaries of space. Yet shifting our position carries us through doorways and around objects, changing our perceptions of space. We may move to a shady porch, descend to a cool lower floor, or leave the house entirely and go out under the trees on a warm summer afternoon. In winter, we may go upstairs for the rising heat or gather close to a fireplace. Each of these small migrations not only promises more comfort elsewhere, it rhythmically animates passages that vary with time and season.

Troy Chattariyangkul, an art student, has provided maps and a firsthand account of his passages through his family house in Monterey Park, California. Different seasons evoke separate passages, using up more or less of the house and its surroundings.

> In the cold winter season I usually move around from the living room to the kitchen a lot. My family and I usually stay close together for warmth. I enjoy this as well because we would usually watch a movie together while eating popcorn.
>
> During summer I usually move from the family room to my bedroom, back and forth all day because it is nice and cool in my room as well as the family room. The feeling I get from these two

House Migrations: Winter, summer, and special holidays. (Drawings by Troy Chattariyangkul.)

rooms is pleasant because I can keep cool while watching TV or even reading a book.

Special holidays are a different story. When all my relatives come over for Thanksgiving, I usually move around the whole entire house, even to the den where I usually don't want to go because it is really cold in there all year round. Usually I really hate it when I have to go in there to get something but I'm forced to.

Adaptive migrations can fill a space at one time and leave it empty at another. The rooms of a house can thus pass in and out of existence, appearing and disappearing, alternately changing their qualities for comfort and choice. To understand their whole meaning we need to live in the house for a while.

TRANSFORMATION

Clothing is our most personal shelter, protecting our bodies from the changes of weather and elements. Like migration, clothing is not usually considered a dwelling adjustment and yet we use it in response to changes both inside and outside our houses. As the days and seasons pass, so our wardrobe changes, altering our look and perhaps even our frame of mind. These changes correspond with the climate of a particular place. In fact, we may so equate a change of wardrobe with seasons that people who, for whatever reason, do not make the change at the appropriate time are considered out of style, or even strange and outlandish.

Deciduous trees adjust a dwelling to the seasons, needing little attention from us. In winter, the leaves are gone, and a thin network of branches and twigs allows the sun's warming rays to pass. Spring flowers cheer us following a long gray winter and, after the flowers, the fruit provides both color and the promise of harvest. The dense leaves of summer shield houses and yards from the baking-hot rays of the sun. The yellows, reds, and golds of autumn hold forth a promise: falling leaves will once again provide a warm blanket for our gardens and clear-

ance for the sun's light and heat to reach our windows throughout the short winter days. Each season not only adapts the shelter but also changes the proportions of space.

Clothing: An expression of seasons and culture; Vienna and Los Angeles.

Houses themselves can be adjusted to seasonal change. A house generally has a basic configuration to match climate and culture. Still, for year-round comfort, some changes are essential; modest or dramatic, subtle or obvious, they are always temporary. These are the customarily repeated alterations that we make to steady our dwellings. Such adaptations are usually matched by regular fluctuations of space and living patterns.

Cherry Trees: A street in
the Slovak village of Prievoz;
winter and summer.

Windows: Open to the garden
on a warm summer day in
Saintes, France.

One very simple adjustment is as direct and uncomplicated as opening or closing a window. Windows, it is said, offer a glimpse into the soul of a house. Surely they provide important clues to the life of those who spend time in the place. The continual adjustment of sashes, curtains, and shades provides a way to darken or lighten a room, to let in or shut out breezes, and to offer a view of outside life as well: to the street, to the garden, to a neighbor's house, or to a distant hill.

Adjustable awnings and sunshades can totally change the look of a house. Traditionally such adjustments have been made by hand, possibly involving the active participation of a family. More recently changes can be made automatically, driven by an outside source of energy. However the change is made, the boundaries of space are rhythmically altered, seen from both inside and outside the house. And if many houses are involved, a whole landscape may come alive.

METABOLISM

The term "metabolism" as used here means all processes by which fuel is burned whether inside our body or in a remote power plant. The most traditional and romantic of all metabolic adaptations is the fireplace. From outside the house, a chimney is symbolic of

Automatically Adjustable Sunshades: The "M-House," Gorman, California. Designed by Michael Jantzen. (Photo supplied by Michael Jantzen.)

"home," usually treated architecturally with some care. Inside, the hearth is a time-honored center of family life. With the exception of the kitchen hearth, where cooking traditionally went on all the time, the space of the hearth changes seasonally, holding the family for winter warmth and storytelling, then releasing its hold in summer.

Only in its latest mechanical forms have we become particularly dependent on metabolism, nearly to the exclusion of other adaptive modes. We can now condition interior spaces uniformly regardless of place or climate. Despite individual preferences, identical conditions persist.

Chimney: A symbol of hearth and home in Williamsburg, Virginia.

Unlike the traditional fireplace, our modern sources of comfort can be invisible. The manufacture of energy is often remote—a power plant hundreds of miles away.[2] Once it has arrived, energy is transferred through hidden wires, pipes, or ducts to different parts of a building. Heating and cooling may go on simultaneously in different parts of a building to ensure a neutral environment. Regardless of inclination, choices about comfort may be designed out of existence.

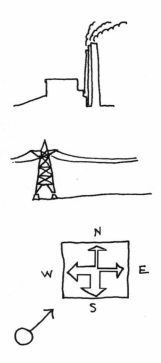

Gone are many of the regional differences that traditionally linked house form to climate and culture. The New England "saltbox" and French Louisiana plantation house were originally designed for quite different climates. Both can now be found across the country, sealed and air-conditioned for comfort.

Gone too are many rituals that originally arose from living in these traditional dwellings. No longer do we habitually gather around the fireplace for comfort on a cold winter's evening, sharing stories or the day's events. Nor, at the end of a hot summer day, do we move to the porch to catch the first cool evening breeze, greeting our neighbors as they pass. We need to look for ways to reintroduce opportunities for ritual into our dwellings.

Ritual

We all have rituals, small ones and large ones, personal and communal. From the way we make coffee every morning to the way we celebrate the coming of spring, our rituals are often a celebration of nature's rhythms—a joyous response to the recurring changes around us. Ritual imparts special meaning to alternations of time and season, setting up rhythms in our own lives that attach us to the places we occupy. Our first responses to change may involve only a search for comfort, but, through repetition, simple actions can eventually be expanded in detail to express our feelings, our delight in a place. It is, in due course, this emergent connection between nature's rhythms and our adaptive actions that can free our thoughts, our creative imaginations.

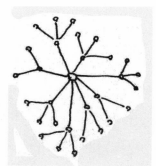

RITUALS OF DAY AND SEASON

Rituals expand the pulse of our life in a place. Taking morning coffee on Vienna's Graben, friends may meet every morning during warmer months, something they are accustomed to doing along

Vienna, Austria: Morning
coffee on the Graben; Feeding
pigeons in the Stadtpark.

Bratislava, Slovakia:
Sledding in winter;
Drawing flowers in spring.

with many others who eventually fill the empty chairs and tables. Feeding pigeons in the Stadtpark brings daily attention and meaning to an otherwise solitary life. Every morning without fail, a lone figure brings her bag of corn to feed the birds, an act that feeds her spirit in return. The more often she does this, the more often the birds are fed and the more often her spirit is nourished.

Ritual is an imaginative re-creation of the rhythms we feel in a place. Children, who celebrate winter by sledding in the snow, may later rejoice in spring by drawing chalk flowers on the sidewalk.

RITUAL ELEMENTS

Parts of buildings can assume ritual meaning. Descending a stair can take us symbolically as well as actually from a private and secret world to a public and shared one. In a house, coming down the stairs can mean joining the family. In a city it means joining countless others. Ascending the stairs completes a cycle by turning the ritual around.

Doors as much as stairs can assume ritual meaning. A door in Suquamish, Washington, is an extreme example. A most minimal act, it stands by itself, no wall around it. By defining an entrance to a nonexistent enclosure, the door symbolizes arrival at a family's domain.

A BACK-PORCH RITUAL

While some rituals seem purely symbolic, others have quite practical sheltering benefits. In Los Angeles, my family sits down every day to eat. But instead of sitting in the same place, at the same table, we move around. The way this happens has been gently guided by rhythmic changes of sunlight and shadow on our back porch.[3]

Almost every day we eat at least one of our meals at the table on the back porch. The meals that we do not carry out to the porch we

Stairways and Doors: Wandl Hotel, Vienna; Ritual door, Suquamish, Washington.

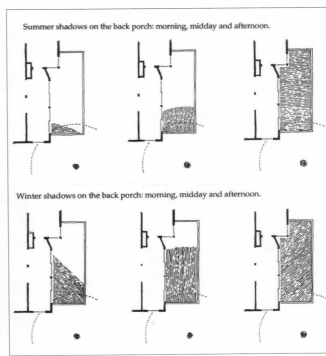

Summer shadows on the back porch: morning, midday and afternoon.

Winter shadows on the back porch: morning, midday and afternoon.

Back Porch: (Left) East-facing with overhanging tree at the south end; (Right) Plan diagrams of shadows cast in the morning, midday, and afternoon during summer (upper) and winter (lower).

eat in the dining room, separated from the porch by glass doors. In and out, throughout a day, we carry food and utensils through the doors.

Two independent sunlight cycles provide multiple combinations of places to sit. In winter we are likely to eat breakfast and dinner in the dining room. But for lunch we have the choice of sitting on the sunny part of the porch. In summer we are more likely to eat breakfast behind adjustable sunscreens in the dining room. But for lunch and dinner, we have the choice of sitting on the shady part of the back porch.

A neighbor's tree spreads over the south end of our porch. To catch the warm winter sun, we move our porch table northward. To sit in the cool summer shadow, we move the table southward.

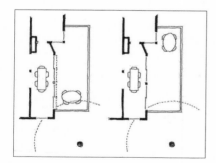

Moving the Porch Table:
(Left) Southward in summer,
under the shade tree;
(Right) Northward in winter
to catch the sun.

Back and forth, once each spring and again each fall, we carry the table across a shadow line. The moment we know it is spring is not exact. We could remember the calendar, but more often than not, on a warm and sunny morning, somebody will say, "Let's move the table." And then it is spring; moving the table has made it so.

Somehow, the seasonal changes and the possibilities they evoke always seem fresh to us. Moving the table shifts all our connections to the house, the view, and each other. The texture of possibilities is rich and rewarding. After 40 years, we are still thinking up new ways of arranging things.

Architecture, by depending too much on machines, has worked against adaptive rituals as a mode of self-expression. This is the result of neither designed nor accidental chaos in the patterns of space and events. It is, rather, the product of rhythms that are too simple and continuous to capture our notice and challenge our imaginations.

The great advantage in machine-made places lies with those who are just passing through, who don't have time or patience to establish a more complex set of connections. This may be helpful to a population constantly on the move. But for those who spend time in these places and try to plant roots, there is a quick decline of original possibilities for choice.

There are many forms of ritual behavior, but the emphasis here is on those connected with maintaining the built environment. In this regard, a time-rich environment offers a complex potential for ritual. Toward this objective, this book first looks to the past and then offers a model for the future. Chapters 2 through 4 analyze three traditional sheltering modes. Chapter 5, by looking mainly to the Gothic cathedral, considers the aesthetic potential of linking ecclesiastical rituals with the complex rhythms of sunlight. Chapter 6 traces a 200-year history of the way rhythms and rituals have changed with the different settings of American life. Chapters 7 and 8 describe the growth of Los Angeles and introduce a zoning framework for solar access and design in cities of increasing density. Chapter 9 extends the idea of urban solar access by describing a dynamic system of zoning that recaptures the dynamism and potential for ritual of traditional means of sheltering. Finally, chapter 10 discusses the promise of a new architecture, one that responds to the rhythms of nature.

2 | Migration

The Roman architect Vitruvius, in his treatise *The Ten Books on Architecture*, included a chapter on the proper placement of different rooms. For example, about dining rooms he wrote, "winter dining rooms should have a southwestern exposure; dining rooms for spring and autumn should face to the east; summer dining rooms to the north." Of course, space was used with unusual freedom in Vitruvius's time; rooms were not assigned a permanent purpose. Nonetheless, his description of proper exposures would necessarily involve seasonal movements from room to room, a different sequence and direction of passage depending on the time of year.

Such adaptive migrations occur in a variety of ways, over miles or only a few feet. At one extreme, people have taken their dwellings with them; at the other, they have simply moved across a room. Regardless of distance or mode, such movements can eventually develop into processions that express deep feelings about life in a particular place. Consider first the Paiute of Owens Valley, California, who maintained permanent dwellings but left them seasonally to migrate across a high-desert valley.

Moving with Time and Seasons

One hundred and twenty miles northeast of Los Angeles is Owens Valley, now the source of much of the city's water. The long and narrow valley runs 120 miles (193.1 km) from north to south. It is contained on the west by the giant blue cliffs of the Sierra Nevada. Twenty miles (32.2 km) to the east, across the perambulations and oxbows of Owens River, are the gentler peaks of the Inyo-White range. Within this dramatic setting, the Paiute Indians once lived in a relatively dense and stable society.[1]

This high-desert valley changes dramatically over the day.

Whitney Portal in the Sierra Nevada.

Alluvial Fan in the Inyo-White Mountains.

Sunrise shadows cast by the Inyo-White Mountains descend the Sierra escarpment before disappearing at midday on the hot valley floor. Sunset shadows from the Sierra crest cool the valley floor before overtaking the Inyo-White Mountains. Corresponding daily temperatures vary over a range of 40°F (22.2°C) or more with the passing shadows.

Seasonal rhythms of snowfall and melt overlie the daily changes of sun and shadow. Each winter, deep snow covers the Sierra peaks, carried there by rising winds from the Pacific Ocean. Each summer, the melt recharges one of the world's great underground reservoirs.

Whitney Portal, topping at 14,500 feet (4419.6 m), is the most dramatic example of lateral valleys that are etched into the Sierra Nevada slopes by melting snow. Precipitation drops off sharply from 40 inches (101.6 cm) on the crest to only 3 inches (7.6 cm) on the valley floor. Trees mark streambeds where water cascades year round, cutting through foothills to meet the Owens River.

The Inyo-White Mountains, bounding the east side of the valley, are older and lower than the Sierra Nevadas on the west. The outline here is not so sharp against the sky. The snowcap is smaller, just a fringe outlining softer contours. Still, the spring melt causes periodic stream action that deposits rich alluvial fans on the valley floor. Today, green irrigated fields define the edge of each cone-shaped fan where it meets the valley floor.

On the valley floor itself, the seasonal Owens River runs between the two mountain ranges. It follows a slow, ambulating course southward through a high-desert landscape. The stream gradient is slight, allowing major sideways movements that leave oxbows along the way. At the valley's south end, an estuary seeps into Owens Lake. The lake is shallow and dries up each year after spring melts, depositing snow-white salts that now blow in the wind from where they are being processed for commercial use.

The action of sun, rain, and snow in the valley creates a highly differentiated ecosystem. Plant and animal communities are narrow in the east–west direction: alpine dropping away quickly to high desert in sharply bounded steps. On the other hand, the same communities are elongated in the north–south direction, running more than 100 miles (160.9 km) in narrow strips the whole length of the valley.

The Paiute took advantage of the valley's richness by migrating. They lived in village groups, each exclusively occupying an oblong territory that stretched from west to east following the direction of greatest biodiversity. Within each territory, a village group moved in yearly cycles. Starting from permanent winter dwellings in the Sierra Nevada foothills, they traveled eastward in spring to spend summer by the river. In fall they continued eastward to harvest pine nuts below the Inyo-Whites, returning to their permanent dwellings before winter. Along the way, they gathered food and materials, always remaining within their north and south boundaries. An account of these travels remains today in an old man's recollections.[2] He speaks to his grandchildren:

Paiute Territories:
(Above) Narrow ecological domains extend along the valley from north to south; (Below) Migrations within family territories extend west to east, crossing ecological boundaries for the greatest biodiversity and choice.

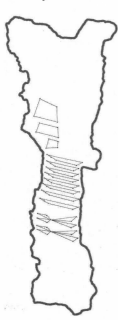

I was thinking of how we moved three times a year. During the winter it is a time of ease because we have prepared and stored our food supply and the wood for our fires, but it is also a time of inactivity because the ground gets so soft and muddy, and it is difficult and disagreeable to hunt or fish or move about. It is also a time when people cannot get away from each other and difficulties arise. The growling always seems to be worse at this time of year. When things happen it is generally during this restless time of year.

By the end of that period, we are glad when it is time for us to move to the river where it is easier to be together. People live further apart along riverbanks under trees. They are content and busy and don't bother one another and they stop growling at one another.

In fall we move away from the river and into the hills, and everyone roams in search of food. But as this season goes on, the hard work tires the old ones. After spending the autumn at work, the husbands and wives are suspicious because it is so easy to meet others in the bush.

Then, it is winter again.

Moving the Dwelling

Adaptations can involve moving a dwelling from place to place. Fishermen, who may spend months at sea, remain safe inside their shelters as they follow their prey. Retirees drive RVs and campers south to warmer climates each winter. Herders traditionally carry their dwellings along well-traveled pathways over land. Here, consider the Bedouin of the deserts who maintain a nomadic way of life.

THE BEDOUIN

The Bedouin of North Africa and Arabia follow desert rhythms. Having no permanent settlements, they carry lightweight, portable tents, following a way of life that has persisted at least since domestication of the camel around 1600 BCE.[3]

Keeping within their tribal areas, Ruwala families of Arabia spend the summer months near the Mediterranean Sea. In September, they move away from the sea to grasslands where they remain through the winter, camping near wells for periods ranging from a day to several weeks, as long as pasturage and water hold out. In spring, they turn toward the temporarily blooming desert where they find water at oases. Finally, in summer, they return to the coast to exchange surplus camels for grain, clothing, guns, and tent cloth.[4]

The desert landscapes that Bedouin groups travel can be featureless and shifting. Space is vast, the horizon unending. Changes are subtle except where punctuated by occasional and often dramatic geologic relief or rare torrential downpours that quickly transform dry washes into lakes and sere plains into carpets of fresh green.

For Bedouin of the Sahara, sandstorms can have disastrous and disorienting effects. Far more frequent than rain, sandstorms can obliterate not only the sun and the horizon but also all environmental cues. Professor of architecture Labelle Prussin, however, points out that, "[T]he considerable obstacles presented by these sand and windstorms during the daytime hours abate at night. Nights in the desert are crystal clear, even when total darkness prevails during the new moon. Regardless of the time of month, nowhere else are so many stars so visible with such clarity, brilliance, and sparkle."[5] So to avoid the obstacles of storms and daytime heat, the Bedouin often move at night during the cool hours before sunrise under the moon and stars.

Centuries of migration through desert terrain have honed spatial perceptions. When moving by day, the Bedouin are guided by an acute awareness of subtle changes of hue and form, wind direction and humidity, the terrain and scents of the desert. At night, they depend on their gathered knowledge of astronomy to navigate the desert vastness, as well as shadows cast by moonlight and the changing sounds and feel of the land surface underfoot.

When they encamp, the Bedouin vary the orientation of their tents in response to seasonally shifting conditions. During the dry winter and early spring, when sandstorms are most frequent, tents are turned against the winds, and must be strong enough to withstand the storms' gale forces. Inside the tent, "the sturdiest and heaviest artifacts are located on the side of the prevailing winds; beds and the weight of people on them, which contribute to the structural reinforcement of the windward side, are located precisely in response to wind resistance."[6]

The Bedouin's portable tent is especially suitable for a nomadic existence. A lightweight, tensile structure, it is easily put up and taken down. Sewn together of 2-foot-wide strips of woven or felted hair or wool, it is usually black or gray with white cotton edges to prevent raveling. Guy ropes pull outward while six to eight poles push upward to stretch the fabric tightly over a hump-shaped space. When clustered with other raised tents in the encampment, the impression is of camels at rest on the ground.

Inside, the tent space is organized for ritual gatherings as well as for protection. Local customs emphasize hospitality so all tents are arranged for the traditional feeding of visitors. "The tent of the sheik, or chief, is the largest. It has a spacious guest area with a small hearth for making coffee, where the men gather to talk, eat, and smoke. In front of this seating area, the tent is left open facing whatever direction is most convenient at that campsite and for the current weather. . . . Cooking takes place on a larger hearth in the women's part of the tent or just outside it."[7]

The Bedouin attach symbolic meaning to their tents. The tents are carried from one campsite to another on camelback. Once the group has arrived, women, who design, make, and own the tents, do all the work of erecting and dismantling them. Yet when a marriage takes place, the groom is said to "build a tent over his wife."[8]

The symbolism of the tent is carried into modern urban life. Ali al-Ambar, a Saudi ethnologist, is quoted as saying, "The first thing any Saudi does when he builds a new home, even in a big city, is to put a tent in the garden, or a figurative version of it in the house" for the traditional *majlis*, a social gathering for conversation and counsel, and for the powerful, an official audience.[9]

The ultimate symbolic expression of the Bedouin tent occurred during the visit of Libyan leader Colonel Muammar al-Qaddafi to Brussels for a meeting in 2004 of the European Commission. Instead of accepting the invitation to stay in the elegant Val Duchesse palace, Belgium's residence for visiting dignitaries, he pitched his black desert tent on the manicured lawn. Here he slept under the watchful eyes of his blue-uniformed female bodyguards.

Moving from One Dwelling to Another

While some people are nomads carrying their dwellings with them, others travel on a regular basis from one permanent dwelling to another. Lisa Heschong describes the common tradition of a special summer place: "The British in India simply packed up during the hottest months and moved business, the colonial government, and all social life up to hill stations, towns in the Himalayan foothills where the air was cooler."[10] In like fashion, New England families have long found relief from the summer heat by moving away from cities to their cottages in the mountains or along the seacoast. Midwesterners, on the other hand, commonly move to a winter place, a house or condominium in Florida, to escape the worst of the bitter cold.

The Separate Faces of Bratislava, Slovakia

Jana Kepplová, a teacher and translator in Bratislava, Slovakia, describes how, each summer, her family moves from their apartment in a city high-rise to their rural dacha within walking distance of Brezova pod Bradlom, a village in the foothills of the western Carpathian Mountains. She explains that they occasionally make the trip for an ordinary weekend but it is the spring visit that "stirs up the most excitement."

But first I will set up a backdrop for her story. In the bitter cold of January 1993, my wife and I arrived in Bratislava where I began teaching at the Slovak Technical University as a Fulbright recipient. We left in the stifling heat of the following July. Between our arrival and departure, we experienced the joy of an explosive spring. And throughout the 6 months we stayed there, I kept a daily journal from which I have selected a few entries to help explain why so many Slovaks keep a summer cottage.

We arrived when Slovakia, as a separate country, was only 1 month old. For a thousand years the people had been ruled by a series of outside forces, including the Hungarians, Turks, Austrians, Germans, and, finally, the Soviets. When the Soviets pulled out in 1990, there followed a period of adjustment in which Czechoslovakia, as a fabrication of World War I, began to unravel.

There are now two countries: the Czech Republic with its capital in Prague and Slovakia with its capital in Bratislava on the Danube River just 35 miles (56.3 km) downstream from Vienna.

Slovakia is more eastward looking than the Czech Republic. First, it is more agrarian, rural, and even rustic, centering on village life. And second, it is nearly surrounded by three formerly Eastern-bloc countries: Poland, Hungary, and Ukraine. Thus it was more heavily impacted by the 40-year Soviet occupation with its forced industrialization, collectivization of family farms, and mass-housing policies. The consequence is a split landscape of antagonistic parts and qualities.

The climate of Slovakia is continental. There are no maritime influences to moderate thermal extremes. Cold winter winds catch one's coat like a sail on an icy sidewalk. Hot summer afternoons leave people gasping for a breath of air near an open window. But the stunning beauty of spring renews the soul depleted by seasonal excesses.

In the 6 months we lived there, we learned about Bratislava both in parts and in layers of time. Prievoz, an old village now woven into the city's fabric, has a rich ceremonial life. By comparison, Petrzalka, the most recent product of architecture and urban planning, is indifferent to nature and nearly devoid of ritual. There are other important parts of the city corresponding to different eras of construction. But in my daily journal, I compared only these two places. Their contrasting rhythms and rituals provide a vivid picture of the reasons for a special summer place.

> *February 6*
> We are renting a modern apartment overlooking an older settlement. Our own street is lined with other apartment blocks, office buildings, and commercial structures. But in the older place, people live mostly in bungalows with clay tile roofs and stuccoed walls close to the sidewalk. The houses have gardens, now cov-

Prievoz Cottages.

Prievoz Convent.

ered by snow. Nearly all families seem to keep chickens, ducks, and dogs. We hear them, especially the early cocks crowing, through our windows.

February 21
I walked through the snow for an hour today in the old place that we have dubbed "the village." Bare trees line nearly all the streets that are now cramped pathways through the snow shared by cars and people alike. Where I passed in front of one house, a young couple was building a snowman and decorating it with a hat and scarf. Children are everywhere pulling each other on sleds, throwing snowballs, and sliding in the icy streets.

March 14
We now know the name of the village. It is called Prievoz, "ferry" or "ferry boat." The name is left over from a time when the Danube, or a tributary, meandered further to the north than it now does and Prievoz really was an isolated settlement along its banks. Now, surrounded by the growing city, Prievoz retains a village atmosphere. A convent, now seen isolated in the snow behind wrought-iron fences, centers the village. Attached to the convent is a hospital to serve the community and a church whose bells we hear from our apartment every Sunday. We walk to Prievoz daily to shop and take refuge in its tree-lined streets and ancient cemetery.

March 21
Today I walked through the oldest part of Bratislava, up to the Hrad (fortress palace), and looked southward and across the Danube to Petrzalka. This newest part of the city is approached only by a modern suspension bridge. One end slices through the fabric of the old city, separating the Hrad from the cathedral, St. Martins. The other end connects to a continuous and uniformly high landscape of pale gray buildings that reach to the horizon. I have not yet visited this place but have been told that all the

buildings are multiple housing. People who live there must commute daily across the bridge to work because there is no commerce or industry in Petrzalka.

April 3

This morning we took the trolley and two different busses to Petrzalka for a close-up look. The place is designed on the Soviet models of architecture and planning. Thirteen-story buildings are of uniform height and aspect made of precast concrete panels. Ground floors are covered with graffiti suggesting personal unrest, alienation, and uncertainty. Randomly oriented to sun and wind, the buildings stand like featureless monoliths floating in a vast and unattended landscape. We saw people picking their way across spaces without structure or boundaries. There are no gardens. Where spaces are occupied at all, it is with cars that are required for the daily commute.

April 4

We have found much peace in the cemetery of Prievoz. The outside world is barely visible through its trees. Sounds are muted. There is a central path, crooked and uprooted, lined by old trees on either side. Many of the trees are splitting open with age but are constantly repaired with cement. Through their dark branches and decaying trunks can be glimpsed the graves, many with small lanterns to protect candles that are regularly replaced, lighted, and left to flicker in the twilight like fireflies. Tiny gardens, regularly tended by the villagers, surround each carefully polished headstone. The gardens are now being prepared for spring planting of flowers.

April 25

The wind has been blowing hard from the south all week and Prievoz has been transformed. Cherry trees that line nearly every street are now heavy with blossoms. Individual gardens are all sprouting new crops of sweet peas, tulips, and little blue flowers.

Danube River Bridge to Petrzalka.

Petrzalka: Uniform 13-story buildings separated by featureless open spaces.

The favorite color of the tulips is bright red. The red, white, and blue landscape looks quite gay. The cemetery is also filled with new color. It has all happened quite suddenly within the past week of warm breezes.

June 9
Whole families are out in the evenings and on weekends climbing cherry trees to pick the bright red harvest. Some of the fruit is consumed fresh. More, we are told, is preserved for cooking and baking throughout the year. This week, friends and neighbors brought us great bowls of fresh cherries five or six times. We have had cherry compote nearly every night for dessert.

June 10
We passed the convent on our walk this evening and in the garden saw a crowd. They were celebrating first communion with all the little girls in white and the nuns in black kneeling behind the crowd. The streets bordering the convent garden were strewn with rose petals where people, lining the route, had showered an earlier parade.

June 17
The linden trees are in bloom and have been for 2 or 3 weeks. Their flowers give off a fresh, sweet scent that fills the village streets and attracts the buzzing bees, especially in the cemetery where we hear them in the quiet evenings. The linden blossoms are used here to make a soothing, medicinal tea.

THE ESSENTIAL CONNECTION TO NATURE

My journal entries document the three seasons we spent in Bratislava, enough to compare the rhythms and rituals of life in two completely different places. The rhythm of village life in Prievoz is complex. People work daily outside the village, most commuting by bus to other parts of the surrounding city. But in the evenings, on holidays, and on weekends, they also have an intense village

Prievoz Cemetery.

life. Partly it centers on collective actions in public places like streets, shops, the church, and the cemetery. Another part of village life focuses on individual actions in personal spaces, especially the ubiquitous private garden. No single beat seems to dominate life. Seasons, of course, assert a very strong influence; but really it is a combination of natural and contrived beats that offers manifold chances to develop ritual expressions of self and group.

By comparison, the rhythm of life in Petrzalka is simple. Unlike Prievoz, there is little gathered life in the place: no church, cemetery, or streets lined with cherry trees. Just as in Prievoz, people leave Petrzalka daily to work elsewhere. But many commute in isolation by car because the location is so remote and poorly connected to the rest of the city. A single daily measure dominates Petrzalka: to work and back. Otherwise, life is for the most part lived inside a flat like a thousand other flats. There are no gardens or cherry harvests in Petrzalka to remind people of the passing seasons. There is slight evidence of ritual in the lives of people.

Slovaks, of course, understand the forfeitures of life in Petrzalka, and those who can afford it take traditional actions to make up for them. It is estimated that 40 percent of Bratislava's apartment dwellers, including those in Petrzalka, migrate to dachas in foothills north of the city. These cottages, often only one room, are nearly always in a garden. Here, the family tradition of planting, tending, and harvesting fresh fruits and vegetables from their own garden is sustained and bestowed upon children.

A SPECIAL SUMMER PLACE

Jana Kepplová tells a typical story of summer cottages, of longing to be closer to nature. Their dacha has been in the family for three generations. It is a well-built stone and wood two-story structure containing several rooms. The surrounding garden is generous, with space for vegetables, flowers, and a small orchard. She de-

The Keppl Dacha in
the Carpathian Foothills:
Julian Keppl and visitor.

scribes a series of customary preparations for the trip. Her account of the family's migration is filled with references to supporting rituals.

I usually put some old clothes into a pile to be taken to the garden. Some foods in cans and bottles frequently remain in the cottage from the previous year but I always shop fresh for things that cannot be left during the damp winter including flour, rice, pasta, tea, sugar, and salt. I have already bought some seeds or some small plants to put into the garden so I have to convince Julian [her husband, a professor of architecture] that he has to find some place for them in the car. I think he takes it as a matter of fact now, having got used to it. Then we leave our tomcat at Granny's.

When we arrive at the cottage we first walk around the whole garden to find out possible damages and losses from weather and from wild animals as deer that enjoy the delicious taste of our young trees. Next, we install the water pump into the well and start cleaning the place, a job that used to be my mother's but now is mostly mine and sometimes [daughter] Zuzka's. We have to get rid of cobwebs, dead insects, and sometime also a mouse. We wash the windows and the floor and make the fire. Julian makes necessary repairs to the cottage and garden and cuts small chips of the dry wood, which is stored in the shed. The fire is kept as long as possible to dry the damp air and walls. We sometimes heat the cottage even in the summer for this reason. I use the ashes on the garden. And then I start for my beloved job—gardening.

Summertime life in the cottage is uncomplicated and unhurried. Julian usually takes his work with him and Zuzka spends some time outside—she goes for walks and if I am not very busy I can go with her. We have our lunches and dinners outside on a sturdy table made from an old walnut tree. I usually make just simple, easy meals: pasta with all kinds of cheese and sauces, salads or I make soups of lentil, bean, or cabbage—we call them "brown" soups and we eat them with bread. We drink tea made from fresh herbs picked in the garden. I wash dishes outside where they dry quickly in the sun and afterwards we have a siesta. We enjoy the evening until 10 pm or later, watching the sky because all the stars are so beautiful. Julian knows the names of many constellations which I like to listen to but am absolutely unable to remember or find except perhaps the most common ones as the Big She-Bear. We have small talks near the bonfire that perhaps seem boring to Zuzka who may have heard it all before several times. Or we visit my cousins who live in a nearby village. It is a lovely walk, especially during moonlit nights when no torch is needed.

Moving Within a Dwelling

While some people seasonally move between dwellings, others are nomads within their own houses. In such diverse places as Iraq, Algeria, and India, climates and cultures might vary, as do the directions and rhythms of movement. But all share migration within the dwelling as a primary mode of adaptation to climate.

IRAQ

Families living in traditional courtyard houses of Baghdad, without mechanical ventilation or heating, migrate by day and season for comfort. In September or October, they move around the courtyard to rooms facing south. In April or May they shift to the north-facing rooms. In summer there is a daily vertical migration, "the afternoon siesta being spent at the lowest levels and the nighttime sleep traditionally being taken on the roof under the stars."[11]

ALGERIA

Such migrations mean that space is used with a freedom unusual in modern life and in the West. Recent correspondence from Mounjia Abdeltif-Benchaabane, a professor of architecture in Algiers, describes how rooms there have not traditionally been organized with regard to individual use or established purpose.

> A living room becomes a sleeping room at night. Closets are full of mobile furnishings. In the morning everything is hung near windows to air out under the sun before being reused, perhaps in a different room. The kitchen is a multifunctional space. They cook on the floor even if they have modern tools!

A long-established Arab concern with privacy, in conjunction with the custom of migrating through the house, established the texture of some old cities like Baghdad. Since the roof is used for sleeping during nearly half of the year and the privacy of the family at night is fundamental, no house could look down upon its neighbor nor could one house look into the courtyard of another. The result was an effective building height control with advantages for solar access; no house could overshadow another, thus assuring wintertime light and heat to upper living spaces.

INDIA

Similar migrations and freedom of spatial use are found in the *haveli*, the traditional courtyard houses of Rajasthan, the northwesternmost state of India. This driest part of India has very little rainfall with hot summers and mild winters. Days are hot for most of the year, but nights can be quite cold.

Orientation of the house and street is important to maintaining comfort. In Rajasthani towns such as Jaisalmer, urban houses are usually narrow and deep, sharing the long wall. The street usually

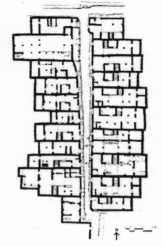

Street Layout in Jaisalmer, Rajasthan: The north–south-running street assures that only a narrow front of each house is exposed to the most critical summer sun that comes mainly from the east and west. Tall houses facing each other across the narrow street also provide a mutual shield. (*Paradigms of Indian Architecture* by G. H. R. Tillotson 1998, 162.)

runs north and south, thus only the narrow face of the house is exposed to the critical summer heat gain from the east and west. The result is a much cooler interior than outside in the street during the oppressive summer.

As in Iraq and Algeria, the traditional houses of Rajasthan generally have two or more stories and are built around a central courtyard. Flat terraces occur at the roof and at intermediate floor levels. The family lives at different levels in the house during separate times of the day and seasons of the year.

The typical urban house of Jaisalmer draws its sustenance from the courtyard, usually the most complex part of the house because it connects other spaces both horizontally and vertically. The lower levels are closed for privacy from the street, but as one moves upward, each successive level is more open to sunlight and air. Besides being open to the central courtyard, upper-level spaces are also open to private roof terraces. "These terraces are almost like courtyards at different floor levels, since they are designed spaces and not left-out roofs." [12]

Studies of sunlight entering interior courtyards and adjacent spaces show important seasonal differences from floor to floor. Only the midday summer sun is high enough in the sky to reach deep into the tall central court. There, at the ground-floor level, a small area of sunlight first emerges and takes less than 2 hours to pass quickly across the courtyard terrace where it vanishes on the opposite side. Otherwise, no direct sunshine reaches the courtyard terrace for the rest of the year.

In contrast to the subdued light at the ground

Sunlight in Urban House of Jaisalmer, Rajasthan: Summer midday (upper) and winter midday (lower). The central courtyard extends from ground floor to roof. Two flanking courtyards occur only at the upper stories. (Computer generation by Kavita Rodrigues based on a section view of a house in *Paradigms of Indian Architecture* by G. H. R. Tillotson 1998, 166.)

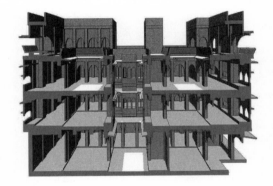

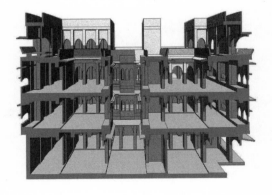

floor, the third and fourth levels of the house are more open and receive direct sunshine year round. This means, of course, that in summer, the two matching courtyards and the rooftop pavilions will be brilliantly lighted and unbearable for most of the day during the hottest months. On the other hand, it also means that they will receive very welcome light and heat during the cooler winter months. Especially noteworthy is that living spaces adjoining the two upper courtyards will receive direct sunshine for at least 4 hours of a winter day.

The second level is where the greatest seasonal change occurs. While the ground level is mostly dark and the upper levels mostly light year-round, the second level experiences rapid changes as the sunlight passes up and down inside the central courtyard during the fall and spring equinoxes. In a yearlong search for thermal comfort, the second level acts as what Labelle Prussin has called a "territorial passage," a spatial counterpart to a pattern of social behavior—a ritual.[13]

The spatial organization of the house supports adaptive migrations. A daily vertical movement sets the tempo of summertime life. During the hot day, the family lives and works deep in the lower spaces of the house that are significantly taller, darker, and cooler than the upper terrace levels. At night everybody moves high up to the roof terraces and open pavilions to sleep in the fresh night air under the stars. Here, the women of the house commonly sprinkle water to cool down the terraces before spreading the bedding. As everywhere, the children join in the watering game and then enjoy skipping barefoot over the now-cool surfaces. Later in the night, the whole family gathers on the terrace to talk,

Daily Migration, Summer. (Diagram by Kavita Rodrigues. Based on a section view of a house in *Paradigms of Indian Architecture* by G. H. R. Tillotson 1998, 166.)

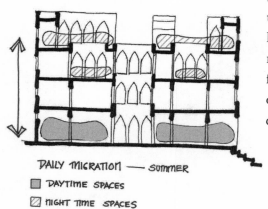

DAILY MIGRATION — SUMMER

▦ DAYTIME SPACES

▨ NIGHT TIME SPACES

tell stories, and share experiences. Finally, they settle in their own places for the night.

In winter, the family occupies mainly the upper floors of the house where they gather to enjoy the warming sunshine. The open terraces at these higher levels are comfortable, the bordering spaces behind arched openings well lighted and warmed. Though sometimes less elaborately decorated than the lower, more public spaces, these upper ones come more alive in winter, animated by the low-passing sun.

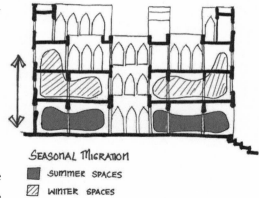

SEASONAL MIGRATION
■ SUMMER SPACES
▨ WINTER SPACES

Seasonal Migration. (Diagram by Kavita Rodrigues. Based on a section view of a house in *Paradigms of Indian Architecture* by G. H. R. Tillotson 1998, 166.)

In spring and fall, as well as winter, the family makes good use of the first level above the ground floor. It does not experience the extremes of either the spaces above or below it. Here, the family can find comfort at "in-between" times, a place that may not be too hot or too cold, too bright or too dark for comfort. At the more extreme seasons, it acts as a place of passage in the yearly cycle.

Moving around is not always the best adaptive strategy. It can be time consuming and expensive, especially when the distances are great or when two houses must be maintained. Still, nearly every climate cycles between extremes. So people have traditionally found another direct way to cope with environmental change: *transformation*. They adjust the place where they are. The result is a broad array of strategies that, like migration, evoke rituals.

3 | # Transformation

THE ARCHITECTURAL JOURNALIST AND AUTHOR, MARY MIX Foley, writes of the "well-adjusted house," by which she means the transplantation and consequent adaptation of European house types to the various regions of North America.[1] She mentions such accommodations as the British Tudor and Jacobean houses to fit New England and Tidewater Virginia, the peasant house of French Normandy to suit Louisiana, and the Spanish courtyard house to meet the semidesert climate of New Mexico. Each of these transplanted house types has diversified our regional architecture and enriched the American landscape. And yet, as each one of us knows from spending time in a place, every house needs continual adjusting, a process that regularly transforms space and ritually speaks of life.

Windows, Shutters, and Doors

"Look at this window; it is nothing but a hole in the wall, but because of it the whole room is full of light. So when the faculties are empty, the heart is full of light. Being full of light, it becomes an influence by which others are secretly transformed." The ancient Taoist philosopher Chuang Tzu thus expresses symbolically the potential for creativity, communication, and interaction radiating from the human heart. And at some level so it is with actual windows. Consider a stylish Georgian house in Edinburgh, Scotland.

THE GEORGIAN HOUSE

Windows tell us of life in the heart of a place. This window that is open at midday may have been closed earlier and may be closed again in the cool of the evening. As it is opened and closed, we learn that somebody lives there and is adjusting the house for comfort.

Georgian House, Edinburgh.

Inside, the window can be seen to have additional means of adjustment. Flanking wood panels open to expose collapsible shutters that filter sunlight. Drapes lower or pull aside to provide still more layers, each independently adjustable.

Doors, like windows, tell us of life in the place. Open, the door catches a cooling breeze while passersby glimpse a vase of flowers on the hall table. Closed, the door is a shield against weather or climate as well as human interaction. As with closed windows or drawn drapes, passersby lose the sense of the heart of the house. And those inside lose their connection with the world around them.

THE SLOVAK FARMHOUSE

Less stylish than the Georgian, but more flexible, are the double windows of a Slovak farmhouse in the Carpathian Mountains. Traditionally built on south-facing slopes, such thick-walled dwellings open to the winter sun, leaving the north wall solid against blowing storms.

Each window contains four separate sashes, hinged on their sides. Two open outward and, separated by the wall's thickness, two open inward. Each sash can be independently adjusted. For example, all the sashes can be either closed or opened. Another possibility is that outside sashes can be either opened or closed while inside ones are opposite. Finally there are different versions where only one sash is opened on the outside and only one on the inside. When combined with degrees of opening of each sash, the possibilities for effective responses to sun, wind, and water are both subtle and many.

THE FRENCH HOUSE

In southern latitudes, where protection from the hot sun is essential, louvered shutters are common. Saintes, an ancient town in southwestern France, has warm, humid summers and cool, wet winters. Here too, as in the Georgian house, a combination of devices maintains comfort. Inward-opening casement windows give protection from cold and rain. Outward-opening shutters

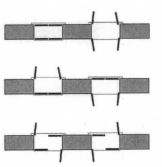

Slovak Farmhouse Window:
Some of the possible
adjustments.

Shuttered Window,
Sainte, France.

provide both sun control and ventilation. Since the buildings of Sainte face each other directly across ancient narrow streets, shutters are also quite useful for nighttime privacy, opening and closing with sunrise and sunset.

When the French tradition moved to colonial America, it was assimilated and changed by the warmth, water, and mud of southern Louisiana. Here, near the mouth of the Mississippi River, French colonists adapted the familiar compact cottage of their homeland. Houses grew stilts to rise above the swampy ground. Broad encircling open galleries sprouted to shelter from sun and rain. French doors containing operable wooden shutters provided cross-ventilation and sun control. Though none of the earliest houses survives in the region, larger and less primitive versions remain prevalent as the *plantation house.*[2]

One remaining example of the French adaptation to a hot, humid climate is Oak Alley, an 1830s plantation house in southern Louisiana. This two-story, colonnaded structure facing the Mississippi River is dramatically approached from the north between two rows of great spreading oak trees. Its 16-inch (40.6 cm) walls are constructed of river-mud bricks. The house, which provides for a comfortable and gracious life, is square in plan, centered by a hall that once served as a second parlor, and is surrounded by a wide veranda.

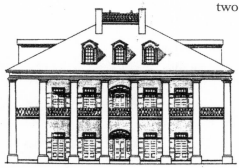

Oak Alley: Southern Louisiana plantation house, 1830s. (From Ubbelohde 1986, 360.) (Drawing by Brian Anderson and Brian Spencer.)

Architect Susan Ubbelohde has examined Oak Alley's complex response to climate. She explains how the house can be made to function as either an "open parasol" or a "thermal enclave" by adjusting louvered doors on opposite sides of rooms and service spaces. One set of doors opens onto the wide central hall that is topped by a belvedere for exhausting warm air. An opposing set of doors opens to the surrounding veranda. Fifteen-foot (4.6 m) high ceilings in

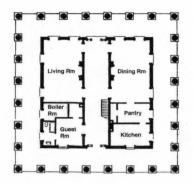 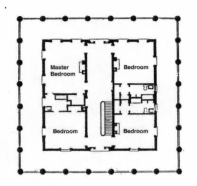

Oak Alley:
(Left) Ground floor;
(Right)Upper floor.
(From Ubbelohde 1986, 360.)
(Drawing by Brian Anderson
and Brian Spencer.)

rooms allow hot air to rise above head height. By adjusting both sets of doors, dwellers are able to open the rooms for summer cross-ventilation or close them against the winter chill. "A second layer of operable sun controls, the wooden shutters on each French door, can be used during those periods when the overhangs do not provide the necessary shade."[3]

THE TURKISH HOUSE

Shutters are often used to stunning architectural effect in Muslim countries where privacy is considered especially important. A Turkish example combines fixed woodwork screens above adjustable shuttered windows. Viewed from outside, the result is a rich composition of varied shapes and textures. Inside, light moving through the screens reconstructs the rooms into conflicting daytime versions of themselves.

Another example, of a single window, includes a central jalousie that slides up and down in wooden grooves against the shifting glare of the sun. In the lower position it historically offered women within a considerable degree of privacy, allowing them to see the world go by without themselves being seen.[4]

A modern example of the Muslim fascination with shutters and light is found in the Institut Du Monde Arabe, Paris. A glass and

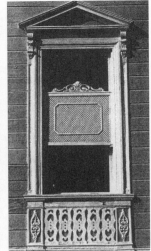

Turkish Shutters and Jalousie. (Photos by Venturi and Hellier in *Splendors of Istanbul* by Hellier 1993, 122.)

steel building designed by Jean Nouvel, the façade is composed of 240 shutterlike apertures that open and close to regulate entering sunlight. From outside, the building appears plain, reflecting the city in punctured squares. But if one stays awhile, the geometry can be seen to change, not in the size of the squares but in the diameter of their perforations. From inside, it becomes clear that what's at work is a system of oculi that automatically expand and contract with the passing sun. The effect is a richly dappled and changing space, transforming rhythmically.

Tents, Toldos, Screens, and Partitions

Movable windows, shutters, and doors change patterns of light and air, thus they alter our perceptions of space. But some traditional shelters actually expand and contract, grow and decay with the rhythms of nature. They do this by means of lightweight and flexible structures.

Arab Institute: Elevation (Left) with oculi; (Right) Interior with moving light patterns.

THE BERBER TENT

Like the Bedouins described in the last chapter, the Berbers of Morocco move from place to place.[5] Along the way, they adjust their tents to match the season. In summer, wall curtains are thrown up on the roof and the tent becomes an open sunshade where breezes blow through. Living space and view expand outward. Families can look inside the lives of other families. Children can run freely in one side and out the other, from tent to tent.

Then in winter, the wall curtains are dropped and reed mats are put over them to break the cold wind and to insulate a contracted living space. The family, instead of wandering freely, now crowds together. Neighbors can no longer peer inside nor can the family gaze out. Children are constantly underfoot. They make noise, screaming and hollering for attention as children everywhere do. They step into food being prepared on the floor for supper. In order to keep a semblance of order, grandmothers tell stories, reciting favorite ones over and over until the weather warms and the winds subside.

Berber Tent: Summer mode, open; Winter mode, closed.

The Spanish House

A Spanish Courtyard House. (Photo supplied by John S. Reynolds.)

Spanish Toldo: Closed and open. (From *Courtyards: Aesthetic, Social, and Thermal Delight* by John S. Reynolds 2002, 187)

The traditional courtyard houses of southern Spain gain comfort by means that transform space by day and by season. John Reynolds has described how Spanish courtyard houses typically use several rhythmic adjustments to nature.[6] One example is the house of Victor Carrasco in southern Spain where extremely hot and dry summers make cooling the major problem.[7] The adjustments he describes modify the courtyard space that centers the house. They also match up with family rituals, private and often joyous.

One of the most appealing characteristics of Carrasco's courtyard, according to Reynolds, is the sound of water. Several small fountains echo softly in the resounding space. The patio floor is made of absorbent brick set in porous mortar. This floor is capable of absorbing water, splashed on it during watering of the plants in the patio and deliberately sprayed for cooling several times daily.

Shading for the patio depends on a movable horizontal white translucent canvas cover or *toldo*. Like a large tree, the toldo casts shade over the entire patio during a hot summer day; unlike a tree, it is swept away in the early evening to facilitate both ventilation and cold-sky radiation at night. Winter reverses the cycle. As falling leaves permit warming rays of the sun to pass through a "mantilla of bare branches," so the toldo is folded back during the day to let sunlight flood the patio; then at night it is closed to retain the heat that was collected during the day.

Adjusting the toldo provides desirable shade but we can also imagine how it changes the feeling of space. Open, the toldo extends the view to the sky, shrinking pupils to pinpoints. Leaves of a tree or of a vine appear in dark outline, wind stirs shadows across the patio floor. The sounds of neighborhood children, passing cars, and barking dogs remind the family of a wider world. In contrast, the closed toldo limits the view, darkens and quiets the space. Sharp contrasts give way to suffused light; moving shadows, to still shade. The atmosphere is more protective, more intimate. Only at the edges of the courtyard, where the toldo does not quite meet the walls, does there remain a trace of the outside brightness.

Such imagery implies an enriched courtyard life. The splashing water not only cools the space but also enhances the fragrance of flowers. Parents spray their delighted children who then take advantage of the remaining water for a round of puddle-jumping games. Birds fly in for a cooling drink, their noise startlingly loud inside the walls. Everything depends on whether the toldo is open or closed, whether it is winter or summer, morning or evening.

THE INDIAN HOUSE

The rhythms of life in southern India are set by the monsoon. While northwestern India is extremely dry, southern regions have a predominantly coastal climate with the Arabian Sea to the west, the Indian Ocean to the south, and the Bay of Bengal to the east. Most of the year is hot and humid with a cooler monsoon season starting toward the end of May and continuing until early September.[8]

Celebrating the monsoon's arrival evokes a series of distinctly Indian customs ranging from small, private ceremonies to large festivals involving whole communities across the country. Activities range from keeping an ear out for the proclaiming call of the first *koyal* (cuckoo) to the grand celebration of *Teej*, welcoming the monsoon. During this time, people adjust their houses and gardens in preparation for the arrival of 3 to 4 months of continuous rain.

Kavita Rodrigues, a graduate student in building science, has supplied a rich account of her life in southern India. She begins with memories of her childhood in Mumbai (Bombay).

Spanish Toldo Viewed from Inside: Open (Photo supplied by John S. Reynolds); and closed (From *Courtyards: Aesthetic, Social, and Thermal Delight* by John S. Reynolds 2002, 87).

As the end of May approached we got ready for the rain by buying raincoats and rubber shoes. I would have my annual argument with my mother, which stemmed from the basic difference in what we each thought was the most important criterion for a raincoat. My mother's was mainly the amount of protection it gave me; mine was avoiding the embarrassment of a raincoat that reached my toes. We generally compromised; I got to pick the color of a raincoat that touched my toes. Once the rain started in earnest, the flooded roads and gutters provided a new game. My sister, brother, and I (and the other children in the neighborhood) would have been waiting for days making newspaper boats. We would keep them on the verandah and spend hours making nicer and more extravagant ones. When the rains began we would then spend hours watching the water flowing down the road till there was enough of a stream to float our boats. We would send our simplest boats on trial runs but when we were able to float the large boats along we knew that the monsoon had finally arrived!

A very important part of getting a house ready for the rains is re-tarring the roofs. In central and southern India along the coastline, houses have pitched roofs covered with clay tiles called Mangalore tiles (after the pattern that is produced in tile factories in Mangalore). These tiles are laid on the roof and the joints at the ridges are covered with tar to prevent water from leaking into the house.

The *dambar-walla* (tar merchant) does the rounds of the houses in the villages, heating the tar in huge vats in someone's backyard or the village square. All the roofs in the area are touched up and problem areas given special attention. Most people traditionally do not pay the dambar-walla until after the first heavy rain, so they can be sure that the tarring is effective. Usually this results in a second visit to redo parts of the roof that are still leaking.

Another important preparation for the monsoon is trimming

all the trees around the house. Strong monsoon winds are capable of knocking down large healthy trees. People reduce potential damage by thinning the trees and cutting away all dead and dying branches. The trimmings are then burned in backyards while children dance around the blaze. The ashes are sometimes used as fertilizer for the gardens in which special "monsoon vegetables" are grown.

The traditional houses of southern India have deep overhangs and shaded verandahs.[9] Some, like the wealthier *zamindaar* (landowner) houses, are usually large with inner courtyards. Other houses, like those of the farmers, are smaller and often do not have an inner courtyard. In these two kinds of houses, people adapt to the monsoon in different ways.

The larger, landowner houses have no need for major changes. Verandas encircle the inside courtyards as well as bordering the entire outside of the house. The outside verandas keep the hot summer sun from reaching the house walls but during the monsoon they get too wet to occupy. Consequently, people migrate to stay dry. Unlike the vertical migrations of Rajasthan to escape the desert sun of northern India, people in the south move horizontally through the house to avoid the rain. Activities that were conducted in outside spaces now move inside to the more protected verandas surrounding the courtyard. When the monsoon is over, the migration is reversed as the outside spaces become useful again.

However, the smaller, farmer houses in the same region sometimes lack courtyards for refuge so a way has been found to protect the outside verandas. Of course, these outside spaces get wet in the driving rain. So to protect them, most people put up temporary screens of intertwined coconut leaves tied to bamboo frames. The result, although on a smaller scale, is comparable to the toldo's shifting effect in the Spanish courtyard.

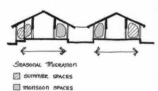

Seasonal Migration
- ▨ Summer spaces
- ☐ Monsoon spaces

The Zamindaar (landowner) House with Courtyard. (Diagram by Kavita Rodrigues). (Based on a section view by Suneeta Dasappa Kacker in *Haveli: Wooden Houses and Mansions of Gujarat* by V. S. Pramer 1989.)

Enclosing the verandas with screens of intertwined palm leaves transforms the space. From an open passage between garden and house, the veranda becomes a self-contained room, cooler and earthier with the smell of matted leaves. When the skies occasionally clear for a short while, shadows have a different quality. Sunlight filters through chinks and cracks in the screens making speckled patterns on the floor. Afterward, when the rain starts again, the space turns back into a haven where people sit listening to the drumming on the tiles overhead.

The palm screens convert the veranda into a protected gathering place where children and adults alike spend their time playing, working, and talking. Kavita recalls the following:

> Grandmothers tell the children stories and reminisce about their youth. Children play games, one in particular called "five shells," which consists of each person taking it in turn to throw five seashells on the ground, and then toss one shell in the air and pick the rest up in different combinations, catching the falling shell as it comes down. Games like these occupy children for hours and keep them from getting under the feet of the adults as they work!

When the rains finally end and the palm screens are removed, the family again spreads into the yard; the veranda reverts to an open passage. All of India rejoices at the end of the monsoon in January.

> People celebrate the festival of "Pongal" marking both the withdrawal of the rain and also the harvest. These festivities are spread over several days and are linked with major house cleaning and burning of junk, symbolizing the destruction of evil. The family gets rid of all the useless things by throwing them into a bonfire that is lit before sunrise to symbolize a new beginning, getting rid of the old. The women and young girls trace decora-

tive designs or *rangolis* on the floors. On the day of the Pongal, newly harvested rice is cooked in homes to celebrate the generosity of the gods. Boys beat little drums called *Bhogi Kottus* and the young people dance around the *kollam* (rangoli pattern) with intricate steps.

Rodrigues's memories of family life illustrate how the traditional interrelation of house design with the rhythms of nature offers rich opportunities for the celebration of life in a place.

A Florida Guesthouse

A more up-to-date version of the adjustable screen is architect Paul Rudolph's design for a guesthouse. Lifted on stilts, and with an open plan, the scheme is typical for a warm and humid climate. What sets it apart is the surrounding cage with screens, adjustable for sunlight and ventilation.

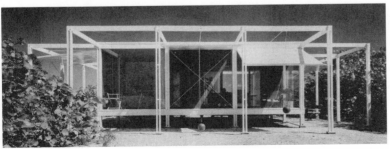

Florida Guest House: Design by Paul Rudolph with surrounding cage and adjustable screens. (From *Solar Control and Shading Devices* by Olgyay and Olgyay 1957, 120f.)

The cage defines an in-between space that bounds the house on all sides. The attached screens are each separately adjustable, all closed or opened in any combination. The screens can thus act alternately as roof, awning, or wall. And as with the Indian porch, the tempo of life in the boundary is set by the recurring changes of climate.

The Japanese House

The *minka*, or traditional house of feudal Japan, is perhaps the most complete example of adaptive transformation. While Paul Rudolph's Florida guesthouse adjusts mainly at the boundaries to weather and climate, the minka adjusts as well from the inside. Teiji Itoh, historian of architecture and city planning, points out that the construction of the minka falls into two main design systems: one fixed and the other movable.[10]

Fixed elements of the minka include a supporting wooden frame and nonsupporting stonewalls. The frame is a post-and-beam system, *jikugumi*, supporting a roof pitched to shed rain. The space below is free to accommodate whatever use the occasion may demand of it. Other permanent elements, such as stone walls designed as wind breaks, and plastered walls and panels, play no part in supporting the roof. Itoh explains: "Because of the frequency of strong earthquakes and the need for circulation of air during the hot, humid summers, load-bearing walls were of little use."[11]

Movable elements of construction that bear no load comprise the *zosaku*, the "fixtures"—the sills, head jambs, rails, walls, windows, sliding partitions, *tokonoma* (decorative alcove), and shelves—all of which define changing spaces within the structural framework. Itoh continues: "The elements comprising the zosaku involve a nailess joint system that allows them to be assembled and disassembled with ease in order to vary the spaces within the structural framework according to the desires of the occupant."[12]

The flexibility of the zosaku system becomes especially evident in the use of sliding doors of two types: the translucent *shoji* that separate indoors from outdoors, and the opaque *fusuma* that serve as interior partitions. Itoh clarifies: "These are alternately installed and removed to meet the tastes of the family as well as ceremonial and seasonal needs. For example, just as the Japanese change the hanging scroll in the tokonoma according to the season, so they also change the shoji and fusuma."[13]

Seasonally moving the sliding doors corresponds with transforming space and the changing patterns of family life. In winter, space contracts and vistas foreshorten. The shoji are closed to the blustering winds while admitting subdued light. Within the house, the fusuma are used to subdivide space into rooms of "myriad shapes" where the family draws together. Since there is no central heating system in the minka, the family share warmth from their collected bodies and, at meal times, they also share the heat from a brazier under the low table. The family can take the opportunity to give news of the day, of work and school, of successes and failures.

In summer, space expands and vistas elongate, even out to the garden. Fusuma are adjusted or entirely removed to open and unify interior space. Without the exterior enclosing shoji, light enters directly and cooling breezes sweep through, setting into motion the entire house. Lacking the wintertime need to gather in small rooms for comfort, family members are free to spread out. In the open space, they hold contact with one another, maintaining awareness of each other's being there. With the passing season and the transformation of space, family life is made over as well.

The Two Types of Sliding Doors in a Traditional Japanese House: (Top) the opaque *fusuma* that serve as interior partitions; (Bottom) the translucent *shoji* that separate indoors from outdoors. The doors slide back and forth in matching tracks mounted above on the beams and below on the floors or they can be removed completely and stored, all in response to seasons or family needs. (Photographs by Yukio Futagawa in *The Essential Japanese House* by Futagawa and Itoh. Chapter 10, plate 6, and Chapter 4, plate 21.)

House Cleaning

Seasonal adjustments of a house do not always occur so dramatically as with the foregoing examples; a house is also transformed and can take on new meaning when people clean, paint, hang curtains, or lay carpets. The altered light through a window, a fresh smell in a room, or a different texture on a floor will create new perceptions, greater understanding. Evdoxia Giovannopoulou, also a graduate building science student, supplied some background for discussion of a house in Thessaloniki, Greece.

She says that, each year, as the weather begins to change, preparations for winter start on October 26, the celebration of the city's patron saint, Dimitrios. These preparations include cleaning the house and replacing carpets that have been removed the previous spring in preparation for summer. Bedding, blankets, duvets, and sheets made of half cotton and half wool are brought out of storage. An extra layer of curtains is added for insulation from cold air leaking through windows. An embroidered velvet cover is added to protect the sofas and furnishings. *Flokati* (shaggy woolen rugs) are thrown on top to create a comfortable and cozy environment inside the house. The family sets in motion the winter practice of opening windows for just half an hour each morning to freshen the air against sickness and the heater's burnt smell.

As the winter advances, the garden too is transformed. Some changes are automatic: the half-meter-deep snow, the bare trees like ironwork against the cold light, and a crystalline cage of icicles hanging from the roof edge. But while some changes happen involuntarily, the family must manage others for comfort. Before the first snowfall, the front door is tightly sealed against north winds, shifting entry to a side door and circulation through the garden. The family makes a game of cutting down the icicles, especially threatening as friends and family arrive for Christmas celebrations.

Preparations for summer begin at Easter time. All heavy fabrics are replaced with lighter ones. Rugs are removed from the floors for easier cleaning, a coolness remains for bare feet coming in from the garden. Heavy curtains needed for winter insulation are replaced by very thin cotton ones letting in more light and guarding the open windows against flies and mosquitoes. Most people repaint their houses using lime whitewash that everybody can afford. This freshens the appearance after winter smoke has dirtied the walls and also enhances thermal comfort by reflecting the extreme summer sun.

The garden is set in motion by summer. The main front door is unsealed for more direct public access, redirecting movement through both house and garden. Without icicles at the roof edge or snow on the ground, the family now removes small furnishings like tables and chairs to the garden. A small bed is placed under the newly leafing trees or under the grape arbor to allow for an afternoon nap. A sewing machine, the washing of clothes, and some cooking are also removed to the garden. Friends and family that during the winter gathered inside the house now spread out under the shade for dinners and for traditional afternoon coffee.

The routine of daily life is often forgettable and so it can be with habitual adjustments to houses and gardens. Yet through matching rituals, the forgettable may carry the unforgettable. From the small scale of private gesture and posture to the grand scale of public festival, rituals bear the memory of a place. But for rituals to evolve, for memories to grow, people must participate in the adaptive process. Our modern lack of involvement is the problem with a third important adaptive mode, *metabolism*.

4 | Metabolism

M

ETABOLISM, A THIRD ADJUSTMENT TO NATURE'S RHYTHMS, depends on the chemical and mechanical conversion of energy. From earliest times, people gathered around fires or huddled to share body heat. Then they learned to bring fire inside the house, first heating only one space where people gathered around a central hearth under the roof and later heating separate rooms with fireplaces and chimneys. Only in its latest mechanical forms of heating and cooling have we become particularly dependent on metabolism, nearly to the exclusion of traditional adaptive modes that once spoke of life in different places. With this almost universal reliance on the same means of interior climate control have come powerful consequences for the world environment, for architecture, and for the ritual use of space.

A Bit of History

With few exceptions such as the radiant heating systems of ancient Rome, occupancy and open fires remained the only metabolic means until the 11th century. Then, medieval advances from central fires under a vent in the roof to mantled chimneys built into the walls of individual rooms brought both health and social change. This change brought lords and ladies out of their common halls, where all had once eaten together and gathered for warmth. Class divisions deepened as owners and their retainers lived more separately from each other. "No other invention brought more progress in comfort and refinement, although at the cost of a widened social gulf."[1]

Not until the 19th century did central heating and mechanical ventilation begin to develop in their modern forms.[2] Rapid conversion to mechanical systems occurred first in the hospitals and public buildings of England and France. In the United States, however, the most important applications of central heating and mechanical ventilation did not occur until the second half of the 19th century when the commercial high-rise buildings of Chicago were built.

From commercial uses, architects soon applied the idea of centralized heating to residential design. An early example is the Glessner house by H. H. Richardson.[3] Built in Chicago between 1886 and 1887, the house was first designed to be well adapted with thick masonry walls on the north side, large windows around a south-facing garden, and a decentralized system of individualized fireplaces. The major living spaces face southward to capture the winter sun. Then, almost as an afterthought, Richardson provided space under the floors for modern ducts and registers that could be connected to a central furnace at a later time. The connection was, of course, eventually made.

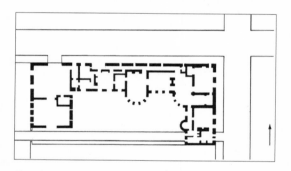

The Glessner House, Chicago. (Drawing by Daniel Wright, architecture student, based on a drawing in *The Architecture of H. H. Richardson and His Times* by Henry-Russell Hitchcock 1966, 106.)

Today, millions of typical builder's houses in the United States depend almost exclusively on hidden machines for climate control. Subdivision layout determines location and trendy styles drive house form. Every developer knows that prospective owners expect to heat the house in winter and cool it in summer just by fiddling with a thermostat. Why worry about taking care and expense with energy-conserving design when the occupant can be counted on to foot the long-term cost of maintaining comfort? Modern dwellers have now mostly lost the time-honored knowledge of how to migrate within their houses or how to transform them. The rituals that once accompanied such adaptations no longer exist to carry the story of the place.

(Left) Frosted Leaves in Winter. (Right) Father and Son in the Snow. (Photo by Mary Knowles.)

Using Our Body's Own Heat

A frosty leaf reminds us that everything in nature responds metabolically to alternations of heat and cold, of light and dark. In winter, the plant appears quite lifeless; the juices stop flowing, the leaves lose color and dry up. In spring, life returns. This all happens automatically with the seasons. We expect to see it happen all around us all of the time.

People playing in the snow on a cold winter day chemically convert energy inside their own body cells to stay warm. Of course, they also wear thick, insulating clothes. But it is what they ate for breakfast or lunch that invisibly and automatically keeps them warm as they play.

Of course to stay alive, our bodies continue to produce heat whether or not the surroundings are cold, so we compensate in several ways. In summer, we perspire and dress lightly. We may seek out shade, perhaps under an umbrella, where we may sit for a while until we get too hot, then dive into a pool for relief. We may repeat this cycle several times over the course

Resting in the Shade Beside Hotel Del Coronado Pool, San Diego, CA. (Photo by Mary Knowles.)

of a summer afternoon, simultaneously displaying our body, our tan, and our favorite bathing suit.

Excess body heat, including that of animals, has traditionally been used to heat houses. Sometimes, farm animals and the family have shared a single space. But often, as in the Greek hills of Zarakas in the Peloponnese, the main living space was separated. As in this example, the hill slopes away, allowing just enough headroom below to shelter the animals whose body heat rises through the wood floorboards to the room above. Combined with the heat from a stove at the opposite end of the house, the family remains quite comfortable throughout the winter. Sometimes, they even sleep directly over the animals to save burning precious fuel in the stove.

Greek Farmhouse on Hillside with Stable Below Living Quarters. (Based on a drawing by Helen Alexaki in *Greek Traditional Architecture, Peloponnese*, edited by Dimitris Filippidis 1990, 25.)

A grander example of body heat tempering a space is the great jousting hall in the Hrad, the fortress-palace of Prague. Today, only scattered groups of tourists enter the hall, perhaps having first walked across the busy Charles Bridge spanning the Vltava River. But in its heyday, eager spectators would have lined the hall's opposing walls for winter jousting. At a signal, starting from either end of the long space, knights on horseback charged each other with couched lances, the cheering crowd supporting its favorites.

Without the heat of the crowd, the knights, and their steaming horses, such a big space would have offered little protection from the intense cold of a Prague winter. Nor would the two fireplaces, one placed at either end of the hall, have offered much relief unless one sat close to the flames.

Vladislav Hall, Royal Palace of the Hrad, Prague, Czech Republic: Once used for jousting, this largest secular space in Eastern Europe now serves for state functions.

We can imagine a more modest example of sharing body heat in a simple one-room building. It is the morning of a winter day. Alone, you may move toward the sunny southeast corner for comfort; but as part of a group, you could actually move toward the colder northwest corner, out of the sun, staying comfortable by sharing collective body heat. As time passes, the afternoon sun changes the places where both the individual and the group might find comfort.

Summer alters the earth–sun geometry and thus your movement inside the space. In North America, on a summer day, the sun rises quite far north of east and sets north of west, although at midday it passes to the south of the building. Thus, in the morning, you might move toward the southwest corner out of the sun, either alone or in a group. In the afternoon, you might move toward the southeast corner, again to stay out of the sun. Sharing the collected body heat of a group for comfort is clearly less effective in the summertime.

Instead of moving people, an alternate technique is to transfer body heat by low-velocity fans. For example, rooms that are fully occupied may produce more heat than required for comfort. The excess heat, when channeled through ducts, can usefully temper colder and less occupied rooms. Although this method requires less moving around, it also offers less variety and choice, less participation in the place.

On-Site Combustion and Decentralized Control

Beyond a limited temperature range, chemical changes in our body cells no longer keep us comfortable and we resort to means of energy conversion that are external to ourselves. Traditionally, this has meant lighting a fire and finding a dependable source of fuel to feed it. Then, because fires can be dangerous when lighted inside a building, they need to be controlled. From a wood fire in the middle of a room to the modern oil- or gas-burning furnace, solutions to the problem of control have characterized architectural styles throughout history.

Open fires have long been with us. Seen in the darkness across

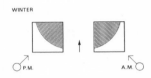

WINTER

Winter Sunshine in a One-Room Space: Morning and afternoon.

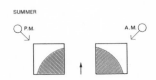

SUMMER

Summer Sunshine in a One-Room Space: Morning and afternoon.

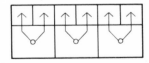

Body-Heat Transfer from Large Occupied Rooms to Smaller, Less Busy Spaces.

Open Fire, a Symbol of Safety and Sustenance.

Czech Kitchen Stove: The Miller's House Museum, Carpathian Mountains, Moravia. Viewed from front and back. (Photos by Mary Knowles.)

a plain or through the woods, they remain today a symbol of safety and sustenance. In some parts of the world, they are essential for life, for warmth, and for cooking. In other places, they are not necessary for life but continue to be used for ritual gatherings. Outside, the open fire is usually easy to control simply by adding more or less fuel. On the other hand, moving the fire inside creates a whole new set of control problems, although it opens new possibilities for a rich social life inside the house.

In the Carpathian Mountains of Moravia, in the Czech Republic, traditional country kitchens all contain huge masonry stoves overhung by a hood that channels smoke safely to a chimney. Here, meals are prepared daily and heavy breads baked weekly for the family; on holy days, hot fruit pastries fill the room with tantalizing aromas. Moreover, the stove centers family life, especially in winter. Children play and grandparents gather to settle their backs against the comforting, warm mass. Some stoves even project through the kitchen wall into an adjoining room where wide

shelves afford a place for sitting or perhaps for sleeping on the coldest nights.

Whether inside the house or out, individual fires require an easily accessible and dependable source of fuel. This can have environmental consequences for a nearby forest. Farmers in the Austrian Alps stockpile wood for both cooking and heating. They draw on nearby forests to supply their local needs. But of course history is replete with stories of people who outgrew their own forest.

Piled Firewood in Austrian Alps.

Where there is no wood, people have sometimes burned the earth itself. Even in modern times, farmers cut peat from the boggy lands of Scotland, digging through layers from sepia to coal-black. It is removed in square "turves," stacked and dried for both heating and cooking. There is, of course, a limit to how often the cutting can be repeated. Each 1-inch layer of peat can take perhaps a century to build up. In that sense it is not a renewable resource.

The chimney long ago became a mark of hearth and home. Sometimes, as in the medieval French town of Loches, chimneys extend inconspicuously, each in its own way, from dissimilar

Turf-Cutting in a Scottish Bog.
(Photo by Mary Knowles.)

Chimneys in Loches, France, (Left) and in Black Hill, England (Right). (Photos by Mary Knowles.)

houses on uneven streets. At other times, as in the industrial English town of Black Hill, the same chimney repeats endlessly on the skyline, conveying the force of mechanization. In either case, whether random and separate or ordered and common, the chimney symbolizes shelter the world over.

Architects have learned to use the chimney and the fireplace as artistic expressions. Chambord Chateau in France is an extreme example. When seen in the distance, it appears like a crystalline uplifting in the landscape. Close up, chimneys crowd together with other devices to make a sort of hanging sculpture garden. Some of the other devices are useful: dormers to admit light, and sheltering domes over small lookout platforms or interior spaces. Others

Chambord Chateau, France.

seem to have no purpose at all other than to complete an imagined picture of opulence and power.

Inside great houses, chimneys connect to elaborate ceramic stoves. Such opulence was typical of royal palaces and houses of the very rich. The stove has no door exposed to the living quarters. It is serviced entirely from a small space behind the walls. Fuel is fed in and ashes cleaned out, servants maintaining the fire that is enjoyed but otherwise unseen and unattended by the elegantly dressed family. Served and servers, the two groups go by each other, mostly unseen, in separate passages through the house.

Off-Site Combustion and Centralized Control

Recent technologies have allowed us to move the fire outside a building, sometimes to extremely remote sites, and send it back in different forms to heat, cool, and light our buildings. The heat of combustion has variously been converted to hot water, steam, and, most recently, electricity for cooling as well as heating. We have gained design choices but we have lost a powerful link with the rhythms of nature that traditional adaptations once celebrated. We do not have to revert to the old ways but, for many good environmental reasons, we do need to find alternatives that offer the same benefits.

Decorated Ceramic Stoves: (Top) Hofburg Palace, Vienna; (Bottom) Zurich Museum, Switzerland.

Today, energy is converted in great power plants and then sent regionwide through wires that hum with inefficiency. Unlike the traditional stove or fireplace, such vast systems, often covering several states, require a high degree of centralized control. And even after the energy gets to its destination, control may be automatic or may lie in the hands of unseen others.

We all know by now that the downside of this practice has been environmental damage, price manipulation, and high vulnerability to system failure and even terrorist attack, but a clear upside is

Palm House: Schoenbrunn
Palace, Vienna. (Photos by
Mary Knowles.)

new design freedom. Architects need not think of the building in traditional terms of location and form, migration and transformation. Plentiful energy frees them to make glass buildings and put them out in the heat or the cold.

Consider the rather extreme example of the glass Palm House at the Schoenbrunn Palace in Vienna. The building is a conservatory, a hot house for plants and trees. One enters from the bitter cold of a January day to find a tropical forest, hot and humid. One must shed heavy winter coats to view the array of exotic plants, completely foreign to Austria. Keeping the plants comfortable requires steam and hot water, manufactured in a separate boiler, somewhere out of the visitor's sight. Today, visitors enjoy this Hapsburg whimsy, mostly ignoring the extravagant use of energy.

Also on the palace grounds is the Butterfly House, kept even hotter by steam from a separate boiler. Here, surrounded by glass, outside nature is canceled, replaced by tropical luxuriance. Hundreds of butterflies fill the air with color, landing wherever they choose on trees and flowers and even on delighted people.

The architect for Haas Haus, an important building on the Stefansplatz in the heart of Vienna, obviously had something else in mind besides basic shelter. Designed by Hans Hollein, its glass

Inside the Butterfly House,
Schoenbrunn Palace, Vienna.

façade reflects the surrounding environment, especially the great cathedral across the plaza. A transparent cylinder honors the corner and marks entry where people can see out and be seen as they climb an elegant spiral stair. The slender cantilever on top is an imaginary roof, not a real one, an invention to augment an effect, not to protect from snow, rain, and wind. Yet the people inside are continuously and automatically protected.

Haas Haus on the Stefansplatz, Vienna: Designed by Hans Hollein. (Photo by Mary Knowles.)

Likewise, people are sheltered inside a Portland, Oregon, shopping mall, a self-regulating machine, independent of time and place. Malls, looking much like this one, appear as well in Tokyo, Los Angeles, or London. Inside, people are free to shop, to promenade, to see others and to be seen, to stop for a snack and chat with a friend, all with utter indifference to weather and climate.

And because modern transportation can rapidly ship goods from anywhere in the world, such places typically offer a broad range of merchandise and produce. Wines from Chile or Italy or Australia can all appear on the same shelf, at any time of year, in nearly any mall in the world.

Shopping Mall, Portland, Oregon.

Distance is not a factor, nor is season. If tomatoes are not available from California, you can try Florida, Mexico, or Chile. If you can't get melons from Northern California, you can probably get them from Southern California. If you can't get a leg of lamb from Oregon, you can probably get it from Australia.

Declining Identification with Place

Treating some prominent buildings with indifference to nature may be justified but what about the masses of unknown and nameless others? Consider, for example, the typical housing blocks of eastern Europe. Centralized energy production has allowed the

Wine Display in Portland Shopping Mall.

Apartment Housing,
Bratislava, Slovakia.

development of countless high-density housing blocks with total indifference to the environment. Every building is pretty much like every other building. No building is oriented, juxtaposed, or otherwise related to its surroundings.

Form is no longer adapted to surroundings, indifferent to orientation. The south side of a building looks like the north side. Since the south side is the winter source of heat and light in eastern Europe, we should expect to see some variety of treatment. Instead, one can go to any number of eastern European cities and see the same kind of housing: block after block, floor after floor, and unit after unit. This estrangement from nature exists everywhere from São Paulo to Hong Kong to New York.

Buildings that are thus indifferent to their surroundings offer no clues to orientation. We may have difficulty distinguishing places, buildings, and even our special place in the building. Inside our apartment or office, lacking exposure to nature's rhythms, we may lose track of time and season. The basis for orientation and choice is denied.

With little or no help from buildings, we usually make a place special the best way we can. Wherever possible, we paint our house or plant a garden. But where we can't personalize a place in one way, we choose another. The problem with some means of affirming identity, as for example graffiti spray-painted on east European housing, is that they can seem to others like an abuse.

Dependence on energy-intensive heating and cooling has freed architecture in one area and trapped it in another. On the one hand, the architect can think beyond basic protection for the body as a motive for design. On the other hand, the resulting monotony does not create any stimulus that might enrich our lives. Modern technology has allowed us to homogenize the world, to act indifferently to the separate rhythms of places. Consider next how those rhythms, especially when coupled with our beliefs, have called architecture to creative heights.

Graffiti at the Entrance Door of Housing in Petrzalka, Slovakia.

5 | Sheltering the Soul

WHILE SHELTERING THE BODY IS TRADITIONALLY ABOUT responding directly to nature, sheltering the mind and the heart can relate to elusive things or events. We may want to express power or wealth, cultural habits or beliefs, or aesthetics. These less tangible goals have both influenced and been influenced by the design of all types of buildings and our ritual passages through them. In a house, the rituals are often personal inventions as, for example, seasonally moving the porch table. In a great cathedral, the rituals are celebrations of shared belief. In either case, rituals very often correspond with the rhythms of actual experience in a place. When the rhythm is complex rather than simple, the matching rituals are more elaborate and tell an expanded story. The result, sometimes quite modest, has at other times been architectural invention of transcendent beauty.

The Two-Door House

Spatial intersections such as thresholds, stairs, hearths, and windows are "territorial passages" between inside and out, upstairs and down, warm and cold. Although associated with sheltering the body, they can as well be the counterparts to a pattern of social behavior, a ritual. It is the repetitive use of such sheltering elements that sooner or later bestows symbolic importance on them. The pattern, once set, begins to have an independent life and power. Consider the symbolic value of two doors where one might just as easily have served.

THE SHAKER HOUSE

"Forever separate, Shaker sisters and brothers passed quietly in the wide hallways."[1] They did not of course live totally separate lives. They shared spaces where they ate, played, and worshiped, including singing, dancing (shuffling or shaking), and preaching. Otherwise, their complete rejection of "every band and tie of the flesh," resulted in men and women living apart. And, while their numbers at first grew by proselytizing, their marital abstinence finally meant their demise.

The Shakers have been considered an American institution although the sect began in England in 1747. In that year, Ann Lee was expelled from the Quakers of Manchester for "entertaining views which were not in accordance with the tenets of the Friends." One such view entailed celibacy, considered by Ann to be "a perfect state in a well-ordered and orthodox life." Another called for the community possession of property. Such views proved to be compelling and in 1774, Ann and some of her followers sailed for America.

Ann had considerable success in America, securing many converts through preaching and healing. By 1787, a Shaker colony was established near Albany, New York. From there her views were carried west and south to establish new colonies. In 1805, "the spirit of unrest or gospel zeal" induced some members to leave for Kentucky and to establish the Shaker settlement at Pleasant Hill. Although the Shakers no longer exist, Pleasant Hill is now preserved as a living museum.

The houses at Pleasant Hill are arranged to divide the sexes. From the outside they appear symmetrical, balanced on the left and right. Two entry doors appear side by side, one on the right for women, and one on the left for men. Inside, the division continues. The doors directed members to separate stairs and thence to divided dormitories. And, while there were some shared spaces in the house, like the dining room, even here the tenets of their religion dictated that men and women sat separately. The two doors at the front of the house distinguished the building as a Shaker dwelling and made physical a core belief of their sect.

THE SUDANESE HOUSE

During the 1980s, a Sudanese architecture student presented a housing thesis, a required project for graduate work. During his final appearance before a faculty committee, he was questioned about why he had provided each house with two front doors. The student explained that it was to accommodate the common practice in his country of dividing houses according to sex. The faculty member persisted that in our day and age, this didn't seem like an appropriate attitude for architects to take. The student responded, with some pride: "Traditionally the women's door is smaller, but I made both doors the same size."

The Two-Door
Sudanese Houses.

THE DOCTOR'S HOUSE

While the first two examples of double doors are driven by religious and cultural beliefs, a third case is more the result of private invention. Built in the 1800s by a doctor in Jefferson, Ohio, this house breaks the rules of classical design. Where the Greeks and all derivative designs have used an even number of columns separated by an odd number of spaces, the doctor used three columns and two spaces. While appearing strange to the architectural eye, it is said locally that the doctor had his reasons. He was interested

Doctor's House, Jefferson, Ohio.

in directing two opposing and separate lanes of traffic: sick patients entering on the right into the waiting room, treated ones exiting on the left directly from his office. Of course, while the device is distinctive, it can count on the common practice in America of passing on the right.

Light in the Church

The preceding examples are of ritual behavior linked with building design but not necessarily with the rhythms of nature. However, when rituals have been architecturally linked with complex natural rhythms, the union creates one of the most compelling circumstances for aesthetic expression.

The medieval church offers an elaborate example of symbolic connections to nature's rhythms. From the darkness of early morning to late evening twilight, the cycle of daily change corresponded with the liturgical phases of monastic life. Seasonal variations were also recognized by separate *horaria* for summer and

Cloister, Salisbury Cathedral.

winter. Thus, according to day and season, monastic activities were organized by "hours."

The daily cycle of liturgical hours provided the most pervasive structure of monastic life, persistent and enfolding. Each day was divided into eight phases, the direct result of fixing the celebration of the eight Divine Offices:

> *Matins*—the darkness of early morning
>
> *Lauds*—the graying before dawn
>
> *Prime*—daybreak
>
> *Terce*—midmorning
>
> *Sext*—noon
>
> *Nones*—midafternoon
>
> *Vespers*—sunset
>
> *Compline*—late evening twilight

Bells rang at these hours, punctuating the daily cycle of the monastery. The passage of time corresponded with repeated passages by monks through the surrounding cloister. The result was ritual comings and goings, back and forth, to pray in the sanctuary.

Passages that measured the day also measured a life dedicated to the service and worship of God.

Although the daily rhythm was most persistent, a yearly rhythm was also recognized, strictly established by seasonal variation. In his *Rule,* Saint Benedict established for his order separate horaria for the summer and the winter. "From the sacred feast of Easter until Pentecost, let *Alleluia* be said always both with the psalms and with the responsories. From Pentacost until the beginning of Lent, let it be said every night at Matins with the second six psalms only. On every Sunday out of Lent, let *Alleluia* be said with the canticles of Matins, and with the psalms of Lauds, Prime, Terce, Sext and Nones; but let Vespers then have an antiphon. The responsories are never to be said with *Alleluia,* except from Easter to Pentecost."[2] To this day, Benedictine monks divide the year with different prayers for different seasons.

The horaria referred to in Saint Benedict's *Rule* were different from the modern hour.[3] Until the end of the 14th century, everyday life was organized according to the Egyptian–Roman method whereby the period between sunrise and sunset (and vice versa) was divided into 12 equal parts called *horae temporales.* As a consequence, the length of these "hours" varied with season and latitude. Day "hours" were longer than night "hours" in the summer but shorter in the winter. This difference was exaggerated in more northern places where summer days are longer and winter days shorter. Thus changing place made time different; changing time made the qualities of a place different. Changing either changed meaning.

The Horarium was also honored in the great cathedrals. In the same way that monastic life was linked with nature's rhythms, so Gothic architects learned to support ritual with color and light. They confined their stained-glass palette to simple and primary colors: grass was green, blood was red, and milk snowy white.[4]

Colors were used in the windows with geometric precision, separated by lead cames, never allowed to fuse. But when light passed through the stained glass and spread onto stone surfaces, the colors softened and melted together in myriad shadings of season, weather, and time of day.

The Gothic cathedral has a cruciform plan that accentuates the complex rhythms of sunlight. The nave extends from the apse at the eastern end, facing the Holy Land, to the great entry doors at the western end. Crossing the nave is the transept, running north and south. This arrangement, which held Christian meaning, also held architectural promise. Cathedrals in northern Europe, where the sun is less intense, were opened more to the light than those in the south. Architects in the north made special use of the different directions of nave and transept. When they let sunlight into the nave through great stained glass windows, it intensified the experience of seasons; let into the transept, it amplified the time of day. The rhythmic counterpoint that we now all enjoy, even if we are unaware of the cause, results from the opposing orientations of these two major spaces. In this way, architects symbolically connected the rhythms of sunlight with liturgical rites.

Rheims Cathedral, France.

Architectural spaces that are elongated in an east–west direction have their major exposures to the north and south, which emphasizes a seasonal cycle of light and heat. For example, in an open street or courtyard, where the containing buildings cut off the low winter sun, most of the space is left dark and cold. The high summer sun, by contrast, lights and heats most of the space rendering it bright and hot. The space can be uncomfortable at either season, cycling between temperature extremes. However, in an east–west space that is roofed, as the Gothic nave, summer sun is mainly excluded while winter sun enters directly through its southern windows. Winter light rather than summer heat

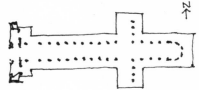

Peterborough Cathedral, England: Typical cruciform plan.

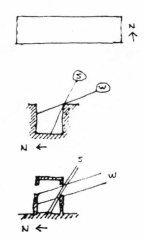

Seasonal Change Accentuated in an East–West-Elongated Space: (Top) Plan; (Middle) Section through open street or courtyard; (Bottom) Section through roofed space.

becomes the dominant force. But whether in an open street or courtyard or in a Gothic nave, east–west elongated spaces emphasize a seasonal rhythm.[5]

Light entering the nave, mainly through the south-facing clerestory, offers a yearlong narrative. The high summer sun barely enters the space, rendering interior surfaces in muted contrasts. In fall, sunlight enters full through richly stained windows, reconfiguring worshipers as they pass below. The brightly colored patterns emerge first on the floor. Then, throughout the fall, they migrate northward across the floor before climbing up the north wall toward the triforium, the arcaded story between the nave arches and clerestory. After seeming to pause there for the winter solstice, the patterns change direction, retreating downward and back across the floor during springtime. The cycle is completed when the patterns die temporarily at the south line of nave arches in midsummer. Then, after pausing, the cycle starts over again.

Understanding this nave cycle takes a year. If one is to appreciate the full and varied richness of its transmutations, one must spend time in the place. Passing through just once, coming at only one season and no other, won't do.

Reorienting the space 90 degrees alters the rhythm of change. Spaces that are elongated north and south have their major exposures to the east and west, which emphasizes a daily rather than a seasonal change. In an open street or courtyard, morning light from the east first descends the west wall to flood the space by midday. As the sun moves into the western sky, afternoon light fades from the east wall before leaving the space entirely in darkness at sunset. Seeking either sunlight or shadow for comfort can involve moving daily from one side of the space to the other. Roofing the space, as in the Gothic transept, gives emphasis to light entering first through east-facing windows and then through those on the west.

Light entering the transept, first from the east and then from the west, tells the story of a day. Morning light enters the transept's east-facing clerestory, making patterns that descend the opposite wall and shrink as they travel eastward across the floor. At midday, for a few moments, the light enters neither side of the transept, momentarily breaking the cycle, throwing all into shadow. Then, gradually, as light begins to enter the transept through the western clerestory, new patterns emerge on the floor, growing larger and more distinct as they resume their eastward movement. Finally, climbing the opposite wall, they disappear with the setting sun. Understanding this transept cycle takes a day. Passing through in either morning or afternoon won't tell the whole story.

While two separate rhythms are at work in the nave and transept, something special happens at the crossing. Where the two major spaces intersect, their independent rhythms of sunlight are both at work. The result is a complex and contrapuntal transformation of space. When combined with the movement of the processional through the tapestry of colored light, the sweet smoke of incense drifting from swinging censers, and the echoing of chants within the stone arches, the effect is indivisible and transcendent.

Of course, the cruciform plan has great symbolic value for Christians. Yet, what the form does architecturally cannot be denied. The nave and transept are different, not just compositionally but also in their response to the passage of time. The Gothic genius lay in symbolically connecting the rhythm of those luminous variations to the rituals of religious life.

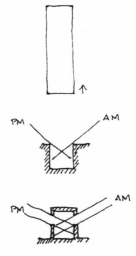

Daily Change Accentuated in a North–South-Elongated Space: (Top) Plan; (Middle) Section through open street or courtyard; (Bottom) Section through roofed space.

A Machine for Living In

While the house and the church have traditionally been rooted in the complex counterpoint of nature, the machine has made our modern life temporally regular and spatially uniform. We are, by and large, disconnected from the rhythms that once gave rise to the rituals of both sheltering and worshiping. There has been a matching architectural celebration of machine-based living.

One reason that has been given is the 14th-century invention of the mechanical clock.[6] Up until then, everyday life was organized between sunrise and sunset, winter and summer. The Horarium sought to cut time into smaller measures, an attempt to regularize the religious schedule throughout Christendom. But the lack of a universal "hour" troubled church leaders like Saint Benedict. The mechanical clock was the first timepiece ever to run at a uniform rate and not be restricted to certain temperatures or lighting conditions. Today, through transmission and adaptation, the clock measures most of our actions, many of our rituals.

Besides the mechanical clock, high-energy buildings have overridden nature and reduced our need for ritual adaptations. This is not to say that ritual has disappeared entirely from our modern lives. Every building has a ritual component: changing classes at school or checking in and out of the factory or office, usually accompanied by some degree of socializing. But most such actions are by the clock. The spontaneity that went along with traditional adaptive modes is missing for most of us.

In fact, during the last half of the 20th century, we saw the near demise of ritual. In the 1970s, anthropologist Mary Douglas wrote about a "mysterious and widespread explicit rejection of rituals as such. Ritual has become a bad word signifying empty conformity. We are witnessing a revolt against formalism, even against form."[7] Douglas was speaking principally about the church but she might as well have been speaking about life in general. In either case, perhaps the reasons that ritual has been rejected are not so completely mysterious as she suggests.

Today, 30 years after Douglas wrote those words, we are seeing evidence of people longing to bring their lives into greater harmony with nature through ritual. Architect Carol Venolia recently wrote of inviting friends four times a year for a potluck with foods of the season. While she says that her intent is for people to "bring something that evokes our place on the year's cycle," she remarks on the "stirred-up" spontaneity of the events. "Each time we gather, I'm delighted by the unpredictable mix of offerings."[8] While this example may seem trifling, it points out an important correspondence. More than signifying "empty conformity," ritual can evoke spontaneity and choice.

In great part, our longing for nature results from unprecedented global urbanization and our separation from the land. In 1950, only New York contained 10 million people. By 2015, there will be 25 cities of roughly 10 million or more, six of those over 20 million. By 2030, 60 percent of the world's people are expected to occupy cities.[9] Consequently, we are fast losing our connection to nature.

At the same time, our hunger for ritual results not only from urbanization but also from the way we make most of our buildings. When buildings isolate us from any environmental change that could summon us to action, we lose a motive for ritual, a stimulus for creativity. Today, we mechanically lighten the night and darken the day, heat the winter and cool the summer. When we so completely override nature, we not only lessen the need for many customarily repeated acts of sheltering but we also lose a creative impulse.

It is becoming the same the world over. Hong Kong is one of the densest cities in the world, and consequently one of the most dependent on the machine. The harbor on one side and the mountains on the other have limited outward expansion. Hence, growth has been directed upward. We excuse this detachment from nature by citing world trade, commerce, land values, and construction costs: all the same reasons used in dozens of other world-class cities.

Hong Kong Harbor.
(Photo by John Knowles.)

Modern urban housing looks the same in Hong Kong as it does in Los Angeles or London. Not only is there a generalized lack of response to ambient climate but also a specific indifference to the directions of sun and wind. All actions in response to natural variation are automatic, mechanical and generally hidden from view.

Perhaps the ultimate machine symbol is the modern office building. It not only works like a machine but also sometimes assumes a machine aesthetic. There are no external variations of

Hong Kong Housing.
(Photo by John Knowles.)

shape corresponding to sunlight or gravity that might cue us as to which way we are looking. There are no internal variations of light, of air or humidity to stimulate the senses and remind us that time is passing. It is an unvarying world of fluorescent tubes and uniformly conditioned air, of cubicles and computers. The most persistent ritual takes people up in the morning, down at night. Otherwise, one can theoretically stay at one's desk indefinitely, enveloped by a monotone behind sealed windows.

So far, this book has been about buildings, but buildings do not exist as separate things. They have a context, a setting with its own rhythms and corresponding rituals. Those settings have changed dramatically with growth. The next chapter traces a history of this change in the American heartland.

Hong Kong Office Building.
(Photo by John Knowles.)

6 | Settings and Rituals

W E DO NOT SEEK SHELTER IN ISOLATION. WE LIVE IN communities. These shared settings provide the larger context for our lives, multiplying and enriching our relationships. They have, as well, their own communal rhythms and rituals that measure our possibilities for choice.

Each community has its own present aspect, the product of the past that has created it. To understand its present, we must understand its history. Planner Timothy Beatley writes, "The essential histories that define a place . . . are not just the built form or natural landscapes; they are the meanings and particular human histories that personalize them. Every community has a rich history and many compelling stories to tell about its past and the former residents who lived, married, raised families, started businesses, and undertook community and civic projects."[1]

Over the past 200 years in the United States, our settings have changed dramatically. There has been a major shift of scale as we have moved from a rural, agrarian society to a highly urbanized one. There are lessons to be drawn from tracing this historical shift. If we can see what we have gained and lost, we might better understand what needs to be restored.

As our settings have changed, so have the connections between nature and machine, between natural rhythms and contrived ones. Life on family farms and rural villages was usually steady, inevitably linked with the cycles of day and season. Natural rhythms offered people endless chances to recite the same tasks, presumably making slightly different choices and learning slightly different lessons each time. On the other hand, in landscapes of rapid growth such as modern cities, people must often reevaluate their constantly changing circumstances. In the American Midwest this change began in the late 18th century.

Ashtabula County, Ohio

Ashtabula County, in the northeast corner of Ohio, typifies the ways American life has changed during the last two centuries. Settlers began to arrive in the late 1700s and, throughout the 1800s, the county gradually filled with small family farms. Villages emerged as complements to the rural life around them, often located near a gristmill or sawmill. Finally, towns appeared "as foreign bodies set down, like boulders on a plain."[2] As people's circumstances changed, they measured their possibilities by a succession of different rhythms.

The northeastern corner of Ohio is a place of transition. The border with Pennsylvania marks the end of the Allegheny Mountains and the beginning of a more gentle terrain. For early settlers (random squatters followed by legitimate buyers) this meant that from here and as far west as anyone could imagine, there was land worth taking.

The region once lay beneath the great Pleistocene ice sheet that extended southward to the Ohio River. The retreating ice left behind it conditions of slope, drainage, and poor soils that were the result of ice and meltwater. Eventually a deep forest of broadleaf deciduous trees developed. Oaks, maples, hickory, and other hardwoods predominated.[3]

The earliest evidence of human settlement in these deep forests is sketchy. In other parts of Ohio, prehistoric "Mound Builders" left behind a few earthen structures dating back to approximately 300 BCE, but in Ashtabula County, there is no record until the earliest contact with Europeans, when French explorers and fur traders filtered into the region.[4] At that time, the Ashtabula River was the border between the Algonquin and Iroquois tribes. They were semi-sedentary hunters and farmers of corn, beans, squash, and tobacco in small clearings along the river.

The British wrested claim of ownership of the region from the

State of Ohio: Ashtabula County, in black, is located in the northeastern corner on the shores of Lake Erie.

French in 1763. During their brief tenure, the British settled conflict with the Indians by agreeing to reserve a large portion of the area for Indian occupancy. However, within 2 decades, the British defeat in the Revolutionary War saw ownership pass to a new nation eager to expand. Indian rights were ignored as the Midwest was opened to successive waves of settlers from the east.

American land companies in New England sowed the first seeds of change in Ohio soil. In 1795, in meeting rooms far from the wilderness, the Connecticut Land Company set down rules for the orderly survey, sale, and settlement of land purchased in great tracts from the federal government. Each member of the Company contracted for a different township.[5]

The contract for Ashtabula County was typical. The articles allowed for " a survey of lands to be made into [square] townships containing each sixteen thousand acres [6,480 ha]; to fix on a township in which the first settlement shall be made, to survey the township thus into lots and to sell such lots to actual settlers only; to erect in said township a sawmill and a gristmill at the expense of the company and to lay out and to sell five other townships to actual settlers only."[6]

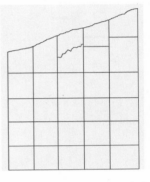

Ashtabula County: Divided into townships.

When the first settlers arrived, they found a land were water is the most active force. Winters are severe with significant amounts of snowfall. Summers are warm to hot and very humid. Over half the annual rainfall occurs in summer, draining into Lake Erie through short streams and rivers. In the spring and early summer, the area is prone to flooding. The weather can change abruptly from one day to the next and thunderstorms and tornadoes are frequent.

An 1815 account tells of a marriage postponed by rain and flooding.[7] The wedding of Reuben Mendell's daughter was to take place just north of the Ashtabula River in Sheffield Township. A friend, Chauncey Atwater, was given the task of walking 8 miles southwest to Jefferson, the County Seat, for the necessary license. He had first to cross the river, an easy task since the river was low. On his return with the precious document in his pocket he got off his course and spent the night in the forest. Next day, when he had again found his way, he discovered that overnight rains had so swollen the river that he was unable to cross at the same ford. He had to take a roundabout course to cross the bridge at Kellogsville, 5 miles upstream. Meanwhile, the wedding party, including the preacher who had come 3 miles on foot from Kingsville, waited an extra day for Atwater's arrival.

The abundant rains that so often cause river flooding also grow rich pasturage. Early farmers planted corn, oats, wheat, potatoes, apples, and garden vegetables in the clay soil, but it was grass that grew best and without human intervention. Consequently, the area became known early in the 1800s for its dairy farms and their production of butter and cheese. Referring to her great grandfather's account books, Rose B. Lawrence, a long-time resident of Ashtabula County, writes a personal account:

> Once or twice a year butter packed in 100 and 500 pound furkins or tubs was taken to Ithaca and New York cities, a slow and tedious [trip] by canal, ox team and stage coach—the trip being made in a week to ten days.

Today, much of Ashtabula County remains rural, spotted with the occasional village or less often a town. The land is mostly open with fields, pastures, and woods. However, there are fewer full-time farmers, who may also be working part-time jobs in towns. Wells are giving way to municipal water supplies. Regional shopping centers and scattered housing subdivisions are beginning to appear. Water is still a major force. It arrives in long summer rains, carving its way through gardens and pastures before draining into the Ashtabula River. In winter it lands as deep snow, yawning over roads, tree trunks, barn doors, and people. The melting snow in spring soaks the soil and overflows the river.

The Farm

Farm rhythms measured the potential choices of a single family. Daily chores were central to the life of the farm family; within these measured cadences most people expected to find their possibilities for self-fulfillment. The growth of the region presented new opportunities, but they emerged first at the circumference of established life, too remote for most people to be affected by them.

The tempo of the early farm was uncontrived. Clocks were used, but chores were more a function of sunrise and first frost than of wound springs and pendulums. Basic patterns were the result of continuously repeated actions.

Accents in the rhythm coincided with the forward movement of nature. The morning of each day and the spring of each year marked not only the start of natural cycles but also the beginning of separate rounds of work. One round had to be completed daily: cooking, collecting eggs, feeding pigs, and milking cows. Another round was completed yearly: tilling the soil, harvesting the crops, and grinding the corn into meal. Shorter rounds fit neatly within longer ones, each adjusting to variations in the other. Days repeated within seasons. Seasons repeated within years. Years repeated within variations too sluggish for people even to notice that things were changing around them.

Farms, when seen in the landscape, appeared timeless, complete and independent. The essentials of life were contained within the boundaries of each. This self-sufficiency (the provision of food, fiber, fresh water, shelter, and waste disposal) required the ritual connection of five basic parts: land, well or spring, house, privy, and barn.

Farmers first had to clear the land, an arduous task accomplished by the family with hand tools and perhaps a team of oxen. Some woods always remained, a trace of the vanished forest, useful for lumber and for game. Orchards, field crops, and, above all,

The Land.

The Well Pump.

pastures stretched toward the horizon. The few other discernible parts of the farm were clustered near the road, discrete elements in the landscape.

Every farm needed a source of potable water: sometimes it was a spring or river but in Ashtabula County it was more often a well that provided a clear point of origin for the farm, a starting place for laying things out. The well was centrally located to provide water for scrubbing floors and boots, arms and necks, fruits and vegetables; for watering livestock; and for washing clothes.

The early farmhouse was often a two-story wood structure with four rooms. It was high on the south with a porch, low on the north. Here, the kitchen, of all rooms, was the most occupied. Except for the stove anchored to a chimney flue, furniture was shuffled around. The family might, at seasonal intervals, shift something as big and heavy as the kitchen table for canning in the fall or feather plucking in the spring.

The privy was a small building serving as the family toilet. Its location was critical. It had to be close to the kitchen door for convenience, but also at some distance or downhill and beyond the well. Polluted water, no less than a failed crop, threatened the family.

Last was the barn. This was the granary, the storehouse for the

The Farmhouse.

fruits of the family's labors. The barn might have been some combination of buildings, including a silo or corncrib. But their combined function was to store a great quantity of harvested material for people and for animals and, in bad weather, to provide shelter for the animals themselves.

The Privy.

These five parts were essential. None could be removed and any more would have been redundant. They appeared as discernible parts of a repeating pattern in the countryside.

The growth of a farm was proportioned to maintain a family. The family might have added a new house but only to provide for uninterrupted succession. A firsthand account by Evelyn Lillie Austin records how five generations of her family have occupied the same two houses on a farm near Gageville, Ohio:

The Barn.

> My story begins on October 3, 1883. My grandparents,
> Sidney and Phebe, were married that day . . . and
> after completion [of a new house] spent their
> entire married life there.
>
> My father Harry was their first child . . .

SETTINGS AND RITUALS

Lillie Farm Houses.

[and when he] married Esther Carlson, another new home was constructed on the same property. I was their first child followed by my brother Maynard. [Maynard and I] grew up living very close to our grandparents and [to our] cousins up the road. . . .

When Maynard married Lois Hayes in 1944, Grandma, now widowed, moved in with [my parents] and Maynard took over the vacated house. Grandfather Sidney and my father Harry [had been] partners in farming this property. [Then it was] Harry and Maynard.

Maynard is still farming the land. After Esther's death, Maynard [and Lois] moved in with Harry. . . .

Duane [their second child] married and moved into the original homestead [where the fifth generation is now growing up].

Those families still live there.

Maynard and Lois Lillie are still fulltime farmers. Their days start early and end late. They milk their own cows, feed their own chickens. A sign in front of the house advertises "Lillie White Eggs." Their son's job is in the city but he still works on the farm part-time during the busiest seasons. Maynard says their grandson declares his intention "to be a farmer just like you, Grandpa" but adds rather sadly, "He probably won't."

For 120 years, stewardship of the Lillie farm was thus maintained, a continuity of recited actions linking the family to the farm. Care for the earth was measured by day, by season, and by generation. But today, while the region remains mostly rural, traditional family farms are fast disappearing, replaced by more specialized, highly mechanized farms.

The Village

Throughout the 19th century, villages arose as markets. Farmers needed a place to buy and sell crops and livestock and to buy things they could not provide for themselves. Villages appeared at the crossing of section roads, often near gristmills or sawmills on rivers. The early village might have contained a school, a church, a general store, a post office, a blacksmith shop, a cooper's shed, and, possibly, a factory for tanning hides or making cheese.

Village rhythms measured the possibilities of a few households, clustered to support the rural life around them. Traditional bonds of kinship were somewhat loosened to include outside relationships. Still, people knew one another by name and were interested in each other's histories. They had their quarrels and usually settled them. They helped one another, and if anything unusual happened, they banded together.

There were accents in village life that did not appear in the rhythms of a farm. Many resulted from collective enterprises that extended beyond the village itself. On Sundays or on special holidays, families from surrounding farms flocked to the village and stood around in the park with its maple trees. From here, they crossed the road to the church or to the store where they peeped through the windows at shoes or cloth from New York. Election days marked a political cycle in which the exchange or affirmation of ideas could affect unseen others.

The repeating patterns of village life, like those of the farm, had multiple layers. There were everyday tasks, small and private activities for which a shop, a house, or a garden was occupied. And there were public actions, shared with more people doing the same things at the same time.

Most days in the village were sluggish but the pace regularly picked up when farm families arrived for the excitement of market days, for livestock auctions, or, on Sundays, for church and socializing. There were even celebrations such as the Fourth of July, with fireworks, foot races for the children, baking contests for the women, that both energized and exhausted people. Afterward, they were glad to fall back to a slower tempo.

The village could appear as timeless in the landscape as a farm. One could see all or most of its parts just by standing in place and turning around. There were only a few basic components, but villages could include different kinds and different numbers. Still, the rhythms of life remained familiar, easily recognized from year to year.*

Houses, more than land, were essential to the village, although behind most houses there was a vestigial farm, smaller and less perfectly developed than its rural counterpart. There was a barn and a well. Beekeeping was customary; sometimes there was a cow or a few goats. And there was a garden that furnished vegetables, fruit, and, for festive occasions, flowers. A garden did not provide all the necessary sustenance, so most villagers worked at some additional task. They occupied a village as well as a private household and took responsibility for maintaining both.

Settlers from New England brought the idea of a "village green"

*For this discussion, as for that of a farm, the parts are exemplary, not necessarily chosen from the same village.

Plan of Typical Village, Ashtabula County, Ohio. Drawing by Lauren Chattigré. (Redrawn from *Atlas of Ashtabula County, Ohio*, Titus, Simmons and Titus, 1874.)

to the Midwest. A public place, usually in the village center, was often reserved for common use, undivided and owned by all. Sometimes it was only an expanded crossroads; more often it was made distinctive in some way. Trees were planted for ornament and shade. Under the trees, pathways crisscrossed a flat lawn and came out at streets on all sides. At the edges of the park, statues or cut stones carried inscriptions of dedication, remembrance, and inspiration. Across the streets and surrounding the park were the few other unique items in the village, buildings that focused the collective attentions of people on education, worship, or trade: the school, the church, and the general store.

Village Green: Kingsville, Ashtabula County.

Universal education was highly valued in 18th century America, and the schoolhouse was often the first public building in a village. The early schoolhouse was a one-room affair where the basics of reading, writing, and arithmetic were taught to all grades. One teacher and, perhaps, a young assistant made sure their wards arrived and had a midday meal. Beyond that, they were also expected to instill temperance and respect for authority, all that was considered essential for building a young nation.

Churches were the second most common public buildings and were given a central place in most villages. Often built on the same basic pattern as the school, they were generally sited at the crossroads or across the street from the village green. With their steeples, they were conspicuous, standing out by shape and size from other surrounding buildings. In villages without a church, services as well as public meetings were often held in the schoolhouse.

The village usually had a general store with the owner living above. This was not a specialty shop but provided a bit of everything. Farmers were mostly self-sufficient but they needed or wanted some things that they could not grow or make for themselves. Again, Rose B. Lawrence writes:

The butter, mutton and beef products were exchanged for script, silk cloth, hoop skirts, etc. All linen and cotton cloth was woven at home. Tea, coffee, and sugar were products mostly purchased.

(Top) Schoolhouse: Denmark, Ashtabula County. (Bottom) Methodist Church: Kelloggsville, Ashtabula County.

Often there was a post office inside the store. Mail might have been delivered only once or twice a month, less often in bad weather. Still, people sent and received messages and thus occupied a larger world.

There might have been a blacksmith shop or even a cooper's shed in the village. These were less common, but small machines of various kinds needed attention, horses needed shoes, and, in a place of dairy farms, there was a steady need for repairs to wooden casks and tubs.

Often, a manufacturing plant was found at the edge of a village and away from the center of things. In Ashtabula County it was most likely to be a cheese factory, but there might also have been a sawmill or a gristmill, a tannery, or a carding factory. Some villages had more than one such operation and some had none at all. Most depended on access to ample, free-moving water and, therefore, on proximity to a creek that could be dammed or to a river.

The village grew as necessary to maintain the rural life around it. Since that life was fairly steady, there was little need for indefinite expansion. Houses appeared one at a time, usually built by the family who would occupy them. But occasionally a village family would build a larger house than it needed, or even a tavern or hotel.

The young schoolhouse assistant usually came from a village family, but the teacher might have arrived from a distant town. Lacking a family, she could find room and board in the village, perhaps with a widow trying to make ends meet as both seamstress and landlady. The widow and teacher together made a new kind of household, not a traditional farm family, but a fellowship of mutual need just the same.

(Top) General Store: Kingsville, Ashtabula County. (Bottom) Kingsville Mill.

Like the teacher, a preacher often came from a far-off place. It is recorded that in 1824 Elder Lane of the Erie Methodist Conference arrived to preach in Sheffield Corners only once every 4 weeks. Then, in 1844, a proper church was built. Here the membership grew and by 1875, the "Rev. E. S. Baker, who resided in Kellogsville, arrived nearly every Sunday to preach to a flock of 40."[8] The record does not show where the reverend stayed on those occasions, but a comfortable night in the village would have served him best. And there he might have shared news of the road with another traveler or two.

It is the number of dwellings, more than their size, that tells us most about a village. The farm meant a single continuous ancestry. The houses in a village represented multiple histories. Most of those were complete stories including family, friends, and village life. A few, like those of the teacher and preacher, were incomplete and glimpsed only in passing.

Villages are still seen in northeastern Ohio, "anachronisms in an era of metropolitan expansion and transportation ease."[9] Most no longer function primarily as market places for surrounding farmers. People still live in them, some because their families have been there for generations and others because they are drawn by their quiet charm. But the sawmills, gristmills, and cheese factories are mostly gone. The general store may now feature antiques for weekend shoppers from surrounding cities while the locals shop at Wal-Mart and drive long distances to their daily jobs.

The Town

Lewis Mumford, the 20th-century urban historian and critic, observed that the change from village to town needed an "outer challenge" to pull the community sharply away from the central concerns of nutrition and reproduction: a purpose beyond mere survival. And so it was with the town of Ashtabula Harbor, Ohio, on the southern shore of Lake Erie, that grew under the influence of Great Lakes trade.

Ashtabula Harbor began with a single cabin, alone in the wilderness. Later, a village "with its log tavern, blazing fireplace, whiskey toddy and a rough, hearty welcome from the landlord" attracted traders on the lakes and travelers on their way farther west.[10] Finally, a town arose to meet the increasing challenge of Great Lakes trade. Its 200-year history tells a typical story.

Before the first settlers arrived, early explorers found the Ashtabula River gorge a forbidding place. An early history of the area reports, "Scarcely any place in the country has a wilder aspect than has this very gorge, so full of dark shadows, lined with tall dark pine and the overhanging hemlock which are only made more striking by the white, ghostly shapes of the great sycamores which fill up the valley. A weird, wild place, almost too fearful for human heart to attempt or for human footsteps to enter. Situated in the midst of the primitive wilderness, these deep gorges were still more shadowy than the forests themselves, fit resort only for the wild bear, the wolf, and other beasts of prey."[11]

Ashtabula River Surrounded by Wilderness.

Life in the first, isolated cabin was determined by wilderness rhythms. In 1803, a settler named George Beckwith brought his family to the forested mouth of the Ashtabula River where it empties into Lake Erie. The following year he perished in the January snow while carrying on his back salt and provisions from Austinburg, 12 miles to the south. His wife remained in the cabin, supporting her children by assisting travelers across the stream in her canoe.[12] The family's terrible isolation was finally relieved as more settlers arrived, but wilderness rhythms could not be entirely forgotten.

By 1812, a cluster of log houses marked the beginning of a village. Forests still covered most of the land and roads were only paths broken through the wilderness. The harbor was a mere opening into the creek. But the settlement grew until, by 1836, "407 steamboats and 156 other vessels entered the harbor loaded with coal, iron ore, limestone, salt and pine lumber."[13] Meanwhile, the cold and deep snows that killed George Beckwith now regularly locked vessels within the piers each winter, setting them free to ply their trade anew each spring. By 1837, framed dwellings had replaced log houses. There was still the river with its seasons, but the old village of 1812 had extended up the street two or three blocks. The period from 1837 to 1861 saw the building of an east–west railroad accompanied by slow but steady growth. A town was emerging.

Town rhythms are more contrived, less influenced by nature than those of a village. The Civil War (1861–1865) added the frenzy of rapid growth—a burst of activity based on two new rail lines extending southward. Everyone still had household chores, perhaps a garden to keep. They still went forth every day to work, shop, and meet friends. But wartime connections to an outside world imposed unfamiliar rhythms of manufacture, trade, and travel on top of the older, more natural rhythms. Clocks and compelling schedules led to an increasingly rigid temporal order. An inflexible rule of being "on time" contrasted with the more relaxed and spontaneous attitude of rural life.

The different aspects of a town, unlike those of a farm or village, cannot easily be seen at one time. They are spread further apart. One cannot see all of life's essentials by standing in place and turning around. Still, the town can be explained as being made up of only a few distinct parts.

The main parts of a town number no more than the parts of a village. Lewis Mumford describes them as the *shrine, spring, village, market,* and *stronghold.* But here, within each part, individual elements often multiply and lose their identity. We must shift our focus from things to classes of things, from number to quantity, and from count to measure in order to describe the town's changing connections.

Houses in a town differ in two significant ways from rural

houses. First, each one stands on a parcel of land big enough for growing only a few favorite vegetables or fruits. While each village house gets water directly from the ground, here fresh water arrives by one set of pipes, and foul water departs by another. Behind the house may be a place for a carriage (later for automobiles) but there is no barn, no individual granary.

Second, the individual identity of each house is lost within a uniform design set. Similarities among them can border on near or actual replication. The building, lot, and street all repeat with only slight variations at the hands of different occupants. The result is the anonymity of individual houses but distinctions among groups of houses based on social status, period, or common site characteristics.

Other types of buildings in a town also appear in quantity. There is not one shop or office but many. Like the houses, they do not stand by themselves. The ones that occupy corners may be special. But along the blocks, while each may try for individuality, more often than not the buildings merge into a common commercial theme.

Districts, not individual structures, are the functional parts of a town. Even when there is a one-of-a-kind thing, such as the bas-

Commercial Buildings on West 5th Looking East.

cule bridge over the Ashtabula River in the harbor area, it is likely to fall into a much larger set of related things. The bridge is simply the most distinctive item in a distinctive section.

The districts of Ashtabula Harbor formed around natural features and successive additions as, one after another, farmers sold their land. An 1874 plan shows a critical moment when new growth was imminent. Farms were already being subdivided so that large sets of needed housing could be added to the existing village. The way these additions were made, their geometry and succession, established the future parts of the town and determined their working links to each other.

The central feature on the 1874 map is the harbor with its river and riparian lands. Here, as the harbor developed, the first to be surveyed on the Great Lakes, boats entered the river mouth and tied up, safe from fickle Canadian storms. Loading and unloading were made easy by close proximity to railroad tracks laid on the level sediments of the estuary. The railroads occupied most of this flat land and held it for future expansion.

Stretching westward from the harbor is the vestigial village.

Here, along high ground overlooking the lake, traces of earlier development have survived. There are perhaps 20 or 30 houses, all identified with a family name. Two stores, a school, and a blacksmith shop complete the typical set. The 1874 plan shows the village remaining as one of the parts of a much larger arrangement.

Starting from the village, new parts were added under the influence of war and trade. An early addition, bounded by Walnut Street on the north and Division and Mulberry on the south, expanded the village southward in a regular grid. The opposing streets, between Ashtabula on the west and Water on the east, enclose uniform blocks that are numbered and subdivided for future development. Streets are named but blocks and lots are only numbered. Each new part appears on the map with a separate geometry. The one on low, flat land east of the river is laid out on cardinal points. Another on higher and rougher land west of the river shifts geometry again to an entirely different orientation. Each different part remains visible today, tracing the early steps of growth.

Ashtabula Harbor Today.

Plan of Ashtabula Harbor, 1874.
Drawing by Lauren Chattigré.
(Redrawn from *Atlas of
Ashtabula County, Ohio,*
Titus, Simmons and
Titus, 1874.)

Ashtabula Harbor recapitulates the developing rituals and settings of the region. But here, all the stages can be seen in one place. First, wilderness living must respond to the rhythms of nature. Then village rites demonstrate an emerging community. Finally, the repeated acts of town life are planned to make the fact of countless lives intelligible. Over the course of time, the rhythms of parts within parts are re-created through combinations of independent rituals. The counterpoint shapes multiple possibilities for life in the place.

The City

In 1878, the old town of Ashtabula Harbor officially renamed itself Ashtabula. Later, as Great Lakes traffic faded, World War II industries gave new impetus to growth and the city's center shifted away from the harbor. The city spread outward, typical of 20th-century sprawl. Today, the harbor area is identified as a historic district. Civil War remnants endure, like a house that once served as the last station on the "underground railroad" from which slaves were secretly moved to Canada by small boat.

The change from town to city seems less clear than the change from village to town. In some ways, a city is very much like a town, only bigger. It is still a discrete element in the landscape. Primarily a commercial center, the city has a major business district at its core. There are also smaller shopping and service centers spread to serve local neighborhoods, but people still go "down town."

Perhaps the major difference is in the magnitude and diversity of the "outer challenge" that Lewis Mumford has spoken of as essential to change. A city serves a wide region that often includes several towns. It offers special services not available in towns. Among them are major medical and educational facilities; sports and entertainment venues; regional headquarters for businesses; convention and meeting halls; certain industries, both large and small; warehouses; and transfer points for shipping goods. Growth begets growth and when the city reaches a certain size threshold, it tends to become self-sustaining, circulating money within itself.[14]

It is the change now going on in the world from city to something still bigger that is more dramatic, having greater influence on our lives. The "something bigger" has variously been called "megalopolis" or "conurbation," an aggregation or continuous network of urban communities. To understand some of the consequences of this change, and what might be needed to bring us back into balance with nature, we can look at Greater Los Angeles.

7 | Boundaries and Choices

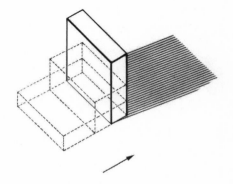

Tʜᴜs ꜰᴀʀ ᴡᴇ ʜᴀᴠᴇ ʟᴏᴏᴋᴇᴅ ᴀᴛ ᴛʜᴇ ᴛɪᴍᴇ-ʜᴏɴᴏʀᴇᴅ ᴡᴀʏs people have identified with the rhythms of nature through ritual acts of sheltering—celebrations of life in a place. But how do they relate to a place of extraordinary growth? What are the rhythms and rituals that foster enjoyment in great cities, that call up possibilities for individual choice and self-expression? Consider life in Greater Los Angeles, a metropolitan region of 3500 square miles (9065 sq km) that has begun to hit limits of space and time. Development has reached the geographical constraints of mountain, ocean, and desert. People are also becoming dissatisfied with the increasing time they must spend on the daily commute. Such limits are already leading to the rebuilding at higher densities of some older parts of Los Angeles as well as other sprawling U.S. cities. The question is how to direct that denser growth to better connect us to nature for energy, comfort, and choice.

While the scale of modern growth has clearly changed, long-established modes of sheltering can offer a useful model for today. First, those modes were sustainable since they depended on building designs and patterns of life to provide comfort, not on energy-intensive mechanical and electrical systems. Second, they offered time-rich environments that called forth ritual modes of self-expression, not impassive responses to experiential monotones. Finally, they linked people to places, to the land and climate. To regain these advantages while providing for growth, we need to explore new urban planning policies that expand choices for designer and dweller alike.

Greater Los Angeles

Los Angeles is a story of water and cars. Water made growth possible in the semidesert of Southern California. The Owens Valley

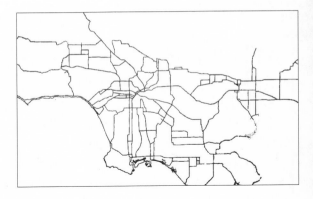

Growth of Major Surface Roads in Greater Los Angeles: Early, middle, and late 20th Century.

Aqueduct was completed in 1913, and with a seemingly unlimited water supply obtained from 120 miles (194 km) away, Los Angeles began to grow. Prior to the building of the aqueduct, local water could only support a population of about 250,000 people. Today, water brought from the Colorado River and Northern California as well as Owens Valley supports almost 15 million people.

Cars allowed the city to spread. The year of the aqueduct, 1913, was the same year that Henry Ford "put his cars on rollers and made his workers adopt the speed of the assembly line."[1] In his novel *Middlesex*, Jeffrey Eugenides describes the effect on workers at the River Rouge plant in Detroit, Michigan. "At first, workers rebelled. They quit in droves, unable to accustom their bodies to the new pace of the age. Since then, however, the adaptation has been passed down: we've all inherited it to some degree, so that we plug right into joysticks and remotes, to repetitive motions of a hundred kinds."[2] Mass-production made the automobile cheap and universally available.

Growth has not followed an even pace. The convergence of water and cars generated a spurt of early growth. Then, after World War II, expansion accelerated enormously, fed by a postwar surge in population and by an influx of people moving from rural to urban areas. Growth continues, fed increasingly by immigration from other countries.

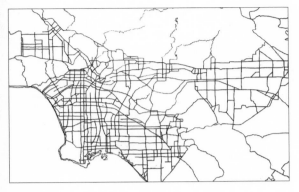

Roads and Freeways

A single century has seen the geometry of the Los Angeles road system transformed. Early roads mostly followed either the diagonal Spanish grid of the original 1781 settlement or pioneer trails through a rough wilderness. Then as more people arrived, the road system became regular, following the orthogonal geometry of the US Land Ordinance of 1785. Three successive maps, starting in 1913, show the progression of major roads throughout the 20th century. The layout of roads has divided the region into ever-smaller and more uniform land parcels. Today, only isolated pockets of larger and irregular parcels remain, scattered throughout the mountains and along the perimeter of the region.

In only 50 years, a system of freeways has extended over the region. But before the mass arrival of automobiles and freeways, people rode streetcars. The "Red Cars" extended 70 miles (112.6 km) east to west and 50 miles (80.5 km) north to south, the most extensive streetcar system in the world. Now, since the 1950s, a vast network of freeways has grown rapidly to serve the same region. The Red Cars have disappeared.

Greater Los Angeles now spreads over several county lines. Restricted in some directions by ocean and mountains, in other directions its limits are vague and unstructured. Coalescing within

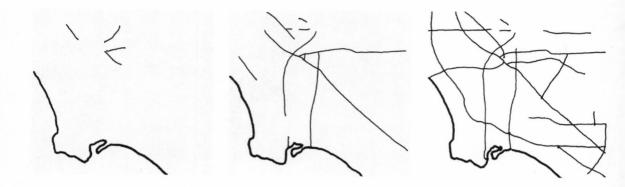

the metropolitan region are separate cities, towns, and even villages, interspersed with large areas of industry, commerce, and service. Some of these parts can be distinguished by building type, wealth, or ethnicity. People tend to live, shop, and seek entertainment in their own neighborhoods but to find work they will commonly travel long distances, even commuting daily for 1 or 1½ hours each way. The consequence is two different perceptions of Los Angeles based on separate rhythms and rituals.

TWO DIFFERENT PERCEPTIONS

The growth of roads has produced simultaneous and conflicting views of Los Angeles. One perception comes from living in a neighborhood. The other comes from driving great distances on freeways. Both are essential for a complete understanding of life in the region.

On one level, generally corresponding with walking or driving on surface streets, Greater Los Angeles has become a collection of separate and identifiable places. Some are cities in their own right such as Santa Monica, Riverside, Pasadena, Glendale, Anaheim, and Long Beach. Others are much smaller, some taking on the character of villages.

When people drive on surface streets, in familiar places close to home, they do not measure distance by miles; instead, they count

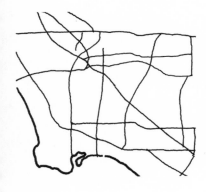

Growth of Freeways
in Greater Los Angeles:
1950; 1960; 1970; and 1980.

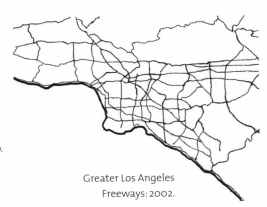

Greater Los Angeles
Freeways: 2002.

the number of tasks completed. What matters is adjacency: the video store next to the dry cleaners, the school near the public library, the grocery across the street from the gas station. Along the way they see familiar patterns, individual buildings with recognizable colors, shapes, and sizes.

Sensations are multiplied by driving on surface streets within neighborhoods. People are continually stopping, leaving, and returning to their cars. They hear outside sounds and smell outside smells. They see and talk with other people as they go about their customary errands. Rituals are intimately connected with the overlapping rhythms of neighborhood life. And walking, even more than driving, gives us time to notice still smaller things: the texture of a sidewalk, the smell of fallen leaves, or a single flower over a neighbor's fence.

In comparison, the daily commute to and from work is usually point to point, from home to work and back without stops along the way. Distances on the freeway are measured in minutes or even in hours, not in miles. Drivers are mostly interested in how long it takes to get from door to door, from on-ramp to off-ramp, from one freeway through the interchange to another freeway.

People traveling by freeway on their daily commute are likely to perceive an expanding monotone with little distraction from outside the car. They shut themselves inside to avoid the onslaught of smog and traffic noise. With the windows rolled up and the air-conditioning turned on, they focus on the radio news, music, or their cell phones. They may taste or smell only their morning coffee steaming in the cup holder by their side. They feel vibrations from the road only indirectly, by extension through the machine. They fill their time with an assortment of ritual activities, separated from a particular place, encircled by the car. But the isolated rituals of freeway driving are becoming ever less satisfying.

Life in Los Angeles depends on both access and mobility, both surface and freeway driving. People need great mobility for a choice of jobs and a selection of places to earn a living. On the other hand, they also need quick and convenient access to stores, parks, and schools. Mostly we have tried to achieve this legitimate aim by using only one limited means of transport: the private automobile. Although the region is, bit by bit, relieving traffic with a light-rail network and a beginning subway, the familiar problem remains. To ease this problem, higher densities are essential.

NEED FOR DENSITY

A change of land-use policies is needed to attain higher densities. Los Angeles is still spreading outward in vast tracts of detached houses at suburban densities of 5 to 7 dwelling units per acre (du/ac) (12–17 du/ha). At the same time, people are recognizing geographical and commute-time limits. Urban designers have long called for higher densities as a way to support diversified transportation and to bring workplace and home closer together. And recently, public officials have joined the call. Los Angeles county supervisor Zev Yaroslavsky has been quoted in the *Los Angeles Times* as saying, "There's less and less land for development. . . . What people have historically come to Los Angeles for is a home with a backyard. . . . But that's not the reality anymore." Higher-density housing, he adds, is the "wave of the future."[3]

The American dream of "a ranch house on a ranch" not only increases the costs in commuting time and pollution but aggravates other problems as well. Los Angeles has long since used up most of its easily developed flat land, including some of our most productive farmland. A NASA satellite study reports that, though cities account for just 3 percent of U.S. continental land area, the land they occupy could produce as much food as the 29 percent of land area now used for agriculture.[4] The loss of fertile soil under cities increases the pressure for production on less fertile soil, leading to overuse of fertilizers and other detrimental environmental effects.

Los Angeles suburbs have now spilled onto mountain, marsh, and desert where growth is costly to maintain. When developers cut into the slopes of surrounding hills, they cause a number of environmental problems. The disturbance of natural water-flows leads to seasonal flooding and mudslides. Wildlife is displaced, pressed ever further into a diminishing wilderness. Wildfires, once an integral part of nature, now regularly threaten neighborhoods.

Building on marshlands upsets essential ecosystems. Intruding into coastal marshes not only creates flood-control problems but also destroys wetland habitat essential to both land and ocean wildlife. The consequences extend far into the future and beyond the local setting.

As Los Angeles moves beyond semidesert into still more arid surroundings, development becomes ever more costly to maintain. Massive amounts of water are imported not only for households but to sustain gardens and golf courses as well. Air-conditioning for comfort in the desert heat uses excessive amounts of electricity.

Denser growth is not only desirable but also inevitable. Under the pressures of increasing population, Los Angeles is in some older parts already moving toward higher densities. New multiple-family housing, sometimes in combination with street-front shops, is replacing dilapidated houses. Older loft-type buildings are being converted to live–work housing, popular with artists and young professionals. But while greater density can better support a diversified transportation system and also help solve some problems of sprawl, questions of life quality as well as energy use remain. Such questions are not unique to Los Angeles.

Worldwide Urbanization

Los Angeles is the stereotypical example, but unprecedented growth is by no means limited to one city or even to the United States. It is a worldwide phenomenon. The U.S. Census Bureau projects a global population by 2050 of over 9 billion people.[5] This increase is a major force driving the growth of cities. In 1950, only 8 countries in the world, half of them in Europe, contained at least one city of 5 million or more. By 2015, 34 countries are projected to do so, on every major continent except Australia.

Such extraordinary growth raises worldwide questions of energy sustainability and life quality. The United States, for example, is reliant on the rest of the world for its energy supply. Net imports of oil are projected to grow to 68 percent of demand by 2025.[6] Furthermore, as people leave farms and villages to live in cities, there is often an effect on the human spirit. Many cities still offer beauty and delight but far too many have lost the time-rich connection to nature that has always given a sense of belonging to and with the places they have traditionally occupied.

Writer Erla Zwingle observes, "Irresistible lure for dreamers, doers, and the desperate, urban areas will soon hold half the world's people." She gives the following numbers: in 1950, only New York contained 10 million people, but by 2015, there will be 25 cities of roughly 10 million or more, 6 of those over 20 million. The number of urban areas with populations of 5 to 10 million is also projected to burgeon from only 7 in 1950 to 37 in 2015. And by 2030, 60 percent of the world's people are expected to occupy cities.[7]*

The impact of worldwide urbanization is not only a matter of number and size but of rate. Never have urban populations expanded so fast. Zwingle comments on Bangkok's transformation within living memory. Older residents recall a graceful town, an "earlier tropical character [of] low wooden sheds, two-story houses with large breezy windows . . . and stretches of emerald trees . . ." now transformed to a sluggishly moving, "thickening, spreading metropolis wrapped in a gray film where air should be."[8]

All over the world, people are abandoning farms and villages for the opportunities offered in cities. Huge numbers of people were not born in the cities they now occupy. Today in São Paulo, a 3000-plus square mile area (7770-plus sq km) of 18 million people, half the population was born somewhere else. Still, the trend seems inevitable. Marc Weiss, chairman of the Prague Institute for Global Urban Development observes: "There's the crazy notion that the way to deal with a city's problems is to keep people out of them . . . but cities are the fundamental building blocks of prosperity."[9] It is clear that the quality of life for most people will be determined by the quality of life in cities.

1950: ● Cities of 10-million or More. (New York)

2000: ● Cities of 10-million or more; ● Cities of 20-million or more.

2015: ● Cities of 10-million or more; ● Cities of 20-million or more.

Urban Population Growth: 1950; 2000; 2015.

*Different sources give slightly different projections, and these change as they are updated. For example, one U.N. website (www.un.org/esa/population/publications/wup2003/2003UrbanAgglomeration2003-Web.xls) projects the 2015 New York population as 19.7 million while Zwingle projects only 17.9 million.

Everywhere, cities must confront the need for higher density. But how is this to be accomplished without undue reliance on high-energy buildings? How is this to be accomplished without losing contact with nature? Future growth can either carry us further from nature or reconnect us, depending on how we direct it. One answer that is applicable to places of density everywhere is to introduce boundaries for development derived from the rhythms of sunlight, a time-rich basis for sustainable design.

The Value of Boundaries

People are generally of two minds about boundaries. The idea of boundaries suggests unwanted confinement, unnecessary obstacles that must be overcome in order to express one's own desires. And yet, thoughtfully drawn boundaries can protect us from the impact of poor, or even greedy, individual choices. Unbounded freedom often results in excessive and even unconscionable behavior that restricts freedom in the long run. Whichever way boundaries are perceived, much depends on whether they are self-imposed or at least understood and accepted.

When people decide to impose boundaries on themselves, it is usually to allow freedom in other, preferred, areas. The medieval builders of Carcassonne la Cité, France, purposely confined life behind massive walls to gain protection from outside armed attack. Likewise, a farmer in rural New York State has built a wooden fence to allow livestock the freedom to graze without having them wander off onto the neighbor's property. Cities often impose boundaries for the common good as, for example, zoning envelopes that define building mass on a site.

When people lived in such rural places as Ashtabula, Ohio, buildings were sited for reasons having to do with climate and convenience. Farmers clustered and even linked their house to barns and other outbuildings for protection from the deep snows

Boundaries: (Top) The double walls of Carcassonne, France. (Photo by Mary Knowles.) (Bottom) A rail fence in rural New York.

and bitter cold. Villagers sited their houses separately, each one free on its own large lot. But urban conditions have led to less independent action. Zoning policies now set the boundaries of development for the common good.

Standard Zoning Practices

Today, building boundaries are usually set in American cities by zoning policy using one of two different methods. The first establishes fixed building-line setbacks in districts of common height and land use. The other, a much more flexible application, is used in what are called "unlimited height" districts, generally zoned for intense mixed-use development. Common to both methods is the concept of a hypothetical envelope setting height, width, and depth. Within this volume, the designer and developer are generally free to act in their own interest.

Building-line setbacks bound an envelope of usable space on a property. For example, a land-use designation for a district of detached houses will usually require an envelope that sets the building back a certain distance from property lines on all sides. The envelope for higher-density housing or commercial development may not be set back at all, or only at front and back, allowing neighboring buildings to run continuously along the street. The volume that rises within setbacks is generally rectilinear, a vertical extension of the U.S. Land Ordinance of 1785. If the imaginary boxlike envelopes could be seen, they would appear to stack themselves along our streets in some rough approximation of the buildings that, under modern growth pressures, will almost surely fill them.

The customary zoning practice of connecting building-line setbacks to land use leads to problems when the use of the land is changed. For example, when an aged area of detached houses is rezoned for higher density, the height and bulk of the new envelope can result in a scale shift that disrupts the neighborhood. The result is not only visually disruptive; it can be socially and economically unsettling as well.

A second method of establishing building boundaries in American cities, also based on the envelope concept, is more flexible in its application. The height of the envelope, instead of being fixed, is based on a ratio between developable land area and the floor area within the building on that site. This floor-to-area ratio (FAR) allows considerable freedom to change building shape. A FAR of 13, for example, limits the square footage of the building to 13 times

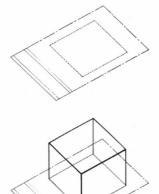

Building-Line Zoning:
(Top) Property-line setbacks;
(Bottom) Volume projected
upward from setback lines.

the developable square footage of land. That FAR may be achieved by covering the entire area within setbacks with a 13-story building. It is also possible to achieve the same FAR by covering only half the buildable site and doubling the height to 26 stories, or by covering only a quarter of the site and building 4 times as high, to 52 stories. Clearly this approach to zoning offers design options that are valuable in high-density, mixed-use development. But there are problems with its application regarding access to sunshine.

As far as solar access is concerned, the difficulty with unrestricted-height zoning is the unpredictability of shadowing effects. For example, in downtown Los Angeles, some tall buildings overshadow an area of two city blocks at midday in winter when people are out shopping and eating.

Orientation as well as height can be critical. The siting of slab-like buildings can have different impacts on the surroundings. A building with its broad flat sides facing east and west will cast a small midday winter shadow, while one oriented broadsides north and south will have an enormous shadow, impacting day lighting, energy conversion, and midday street life.

Regardless of zoning practices, either fixed or flexible, unprecedented growth continues to override nature. Large-scale development obscures natural variation on the land. High-energy buildings mask variety for their dwellers. We need a method of zoning that accepts the common usage of an envelope but with adjustments that reconnect us to nature.

Solar-access zoning opens design possibilities for comfort and choice, for a sense of well-being and joy in a place. It scales new construction to what already exists, avoiding the disruptions of

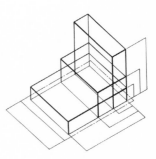

Zoning Based on Floor to Area Ratio.

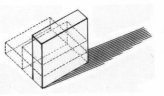

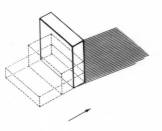

Differing Shadow Impacts at Midday: (Top) Building sited with its broad sides facing east and west; (Bottom) Building with broad sides facing north and south.

great dimensional mismatches. It allows architects to design with sunlight without fear that their ideas will be overridden by future growth. It protects, now and in the future, the rights of property owners to have sunlight in their windows, their gardens, their lives.

Need for Solar-Access Zoning

Interest in solar access generally rises and falls with the perceived security of oil supplies. A brief period of political and economic uncertainty during the 1970s and '80s prompted urgent calls to use solar energy in our buildings, towns, and cities, making solar access a critical issue in the United States. A number of cities and states passed legislation to protect existing solar installations and to ensure continued solar access for future developments. The federal government supported a number of studies to determine the most feasible, effective, and enforceable way to establish solar rights.[10] Then, as oil again flowed freely on world markets during the 1990s, public and political interest waned.

Now, at the beginning of a new millennium, pundits again are expressing concerns about oil. David Goodstein, Caltech's vice provost and professor of physics, has lately written in the *Los Angeles Times,* "Over the last 150 years, we have evolved a civilization firmly anchored in the mathematically impossible premise of an endless supply of cheap oil. Now there is good reason to believe that sometime in the next decade or two, the world's oil fields will start to be depleted faster than new ones can be tapped. When that happens, a gap will begin to grow between the supply of fuel and the need for it."[11] The warning is valid and must be taken seriously, but it is also incomplete.

The difference this time is a convergence of concern for oil supplies (or any other nonrenewable resource) with rapid worldwide urbanization. In this much more compelling context, the sun's energy has again come to be seen as a direct replacement for oil. It beckons as a local alternative for electric power grids that run our air conditioners during hot summer months. But our understanding of solar energy must be broadened beyond photovoltaics (PV) and rooftop collectors.

We need to go further than the perception of solar access as only a way of providing energy to heat, light, cool, and ventilate our buildings. We need to extend the concept of solar access to include a more rewarding quality of urban life based on opening our experiences to complex natural rhythms. This step goes beyond current perceptions of an energy crisis.

If our current energy problems were suddenly solved by some economic, technological, or political breakthrough, and even if our rate of energy conversion could be miraculously doubled or tripled, we would still need to confront the basic issue of life quality. Many have proposed nuclear energy as the answer but there remain problems with its use. It is a highly centralized and inherently dangerous system that is vulnerable to failure, mismanagement, or attack. Nor have we solved the problem of disposing of nuclear waste. Furthermore, assuming any very direct correlation between rates of energy conversion and the quality of life is an incomplete, if not dangerous, basis for national policy.

Most importantly, zoning boundaries for solar access have meaning beyond energy conversion. They have benefits for designer and dweller alike. The zoning necessary for solar access must be understood not as restricting but as liberating. It must be seen as expanding choice both inside and outside our buildings, as celebrating, not overriding nature and differences of place. The *solar envelope*, an alternative to zoning by either fixed building-line or unlimited building-height (FAR), could be a powerful tool to accomplish these goals while still supporting the urban densities essential to the "fundamental building blocks of prosperity."

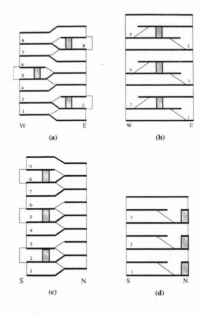

8 | The Solar Envelope

T HE SUN IS FUNDAMENTAL TO ALL LIFE. IT IS THE SOURCE of our vision, our warmth, our energy, the rhythms and rituals of our lives. Its movements inform our perceptions of time and space and our scale in the universe. Assured access to sunshine is thus important to the quality of our lives.

It is a simple fact that tall buildings cast long shadows. A 50-story tower in Los Angeles casts a shadow about 1000 feet long (305 m) between 1 and 2 p.m. in December. By 3 p.m., that building's shadow is close to 1800 feet long (549 m), with an area equivalent to two city blocks. Its leading edge cuts across the swimming pool of a popular downtown hotel, isolating a few sunbathers in a narrow strip of warm sunlight. The rest of the pool area is shadowed, cold and empty.

There is an ethical issue here as well as an issue of quality of life. While I may choose to stand in shadow, I resist a developer's mandating it. If I occupy a building in the wake of another's shadow, I will resist that violation of my right to the sun's light and heat.

There are recent energy-conscious building designs that accomplish their efficiency goals at the expense of their neighbors. A building that publicizes its use of the sun to save energy but deprives its neighbors of the same opportunity is clearly on questionable ethical ground. By using a concept of solar zoning called *solar envelope*, which describes the volumetric limits to development that will not shadow neighbors, we can address the ethical issues of a right to sunshine in cities. We can also reclaim the accents, meter, and tempo of nature in our lives.

The solar envelope represents what urban planner Frederick R. Steiner, in a general reference to planning, describes as "a philosophy for organizing actions that enable people to predict and visualize the future of any land area . . . that gives people the ability to link actions on specific parcels of land to larger regional systems."[1]

A Model for Solar Access

The model for the solar envelope is found in the ancient settlements of North America. Here, a thousand years ago, settlements were laid out for solar access. Acoma Pueblo, located on a plateau about 50 miles (80 km) west of modern Albuquerque, New Mex-

Acoma Pueblo: Terraced houses are well designed to absorb the low winter sun and protect from the higher summer sun. (Perspective drawing by Gary S. Shigemura in *Energy and Form* by Knowles 1974, 27.)

ico, exemplifies such early planning. Rows of houses are stepped down to the south. Walls are of thick masonry. Roofs and terraces are of timber and reeds, overlaid with a mixture of clay and grass.[2]

Individual houses at Acoma are well suited to a high-desert climate. The sun's low winter rays strike most directly their south-facing masonry walls where energy is stored during the day, then released to warm inside spaces throughout the cold nights. In contrast, the summer sun passes high overhead, striking most directly the roof-terraces where the sun's energy is less effectively stored. What's more, east and west walls are covered by adjacent houses thus further reducing harmful summertime effects.

A small roadway separates each row of houses. The resulting

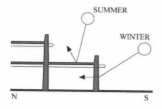

Acoma Pueblo: Low winter sun strikes the south-facing masonry walls most directly; High summer sun strikes the timber-and-reed roof terraces that transmit heat less efficiently.

space between the rows is wide enough so that winter shadows cast by any one row of houses covers only the adjoining roadway. Terraces and heat-storing walls remain exposed to the warming rays of the winter sun. It is this critical relationship of building height to shadow area that presents a model for the solar envelope.

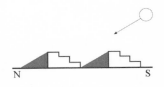

Acoma Pueblo avoids winter shadows by spacing the rows of houses.

What Is a Solar Envelope?

The solar envelope is not a physical thing. It is a set of imaginary boundaries, enclosing a building site, that regulate development in relation to the sun's motion. Buildings within this envelope do not overshadow their surroundings during critical energy-receiving periods of the day and year.

The idea of an imaginary envelope is common to all zoning in the United States.[3] Conventional zoning mostly uses an envelope shaped like a simple box with four sides and a top to establish setbacks and heights. In contrast, the solar envelope is shaped more like a multifaceted crystal or even a series of warped surfaces, generated to follow the moving rays of the sun. Adjacent envelopes can be quite different, depending on their site and particular surroundings. Consequently, buildings made within the solar envelope are more likely to have unique shapes than to repeat boxlike designs.

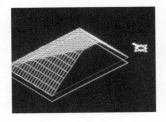

Generation of Solar Envelope: (Top) A solar plane generated for the instant of noon, winter solstice, slopes to meet the top of a shadow fence on the north edge of the site. (Bottom) As the period of solar access is increased, the original plane lowers and other planes are added, one generated by the winter morning sun and another by the afternoon sun. Compass rose points north.

The solar envelope is a construct of space and time: the physical boundaries of surrounding properties and the period for which access to sunshine is assured. The way these measures are set decides the envelope's final size and shape.

First, the solar envelope guarantees sunshine to others by preventing shadows above designated boundaries along neighboring property lines; these boundaries have been called *shadow fences*. A shadow fence is an imaginary wall that rises from a property line. The solar envelope is then configured to meet the top of the fence

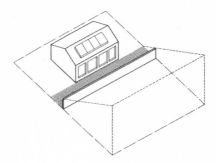

Shadows: (Left) Without solar-access zoning, there is no guarantee of sunshine. (Right) The heights of shadow fences can be set to control the solar envelope, thus the shadowing impact on neighboring buildings, while maximizing buildable volume. (Drawings by Daniel Wright in *Sun Rhythm Form* by Knowles 1981, 122f.)

Shadow Fences: The solar envelope is generated to meet shadow fences that are set according to surrounding land uses and community values. It can extend beyond its own site to meet shadow fences across the street. The shadow fences vary in height, for example, higher for parking and lower for a community park.

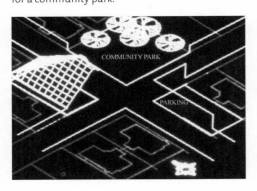

rather than the ground, thus allowing the solar envelope to rise and gain volume. Different heights of shadow fences will affect the shape and size of the envelope.[4]

Shadow fences, being imaginary, do not actually cast shadows but instead allow shadowing of adjacent properties within limits set by community values. The height of the shadow fence can be set in response to any number of different surrounding elements, such as windows, party walls, or courtyards. The height of the shadow fence may also be determined by adjacent land-uses. For example, housing may have lower shadow fences, and thus less overshadowing, than some commercial or industrial uses where rooftop access for solar collectors may suffice.

Second, the envelope provides the largest possible building volume within time constraints, called *cutoff times*. The envelope accomplishes this by defining the largest theoretical container of space that would not cast shadows on neighboring properties between specified times of the day. Cutoff times that are specified very early in the morning and late in the afternoon will result in smaller volumes than would result from later times in the morning and earlier times in the afternoon.

When shadow fences are set at all property

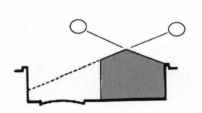

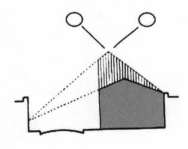

lines (sides as well as front and back), including any adjacent streets or alleys, solar envelopes are shaped with tilted facets defined by the sloping rays of the sun. Each separate face of the envelope is defined by a different time of day or season of the year. And because the wintertime sun angles are lowest, they are usually the main determining factor of envelope form.

A Design Analysis Tool

The solar envelope provides architects and urban planners with a design analysis tool for understanding and implementing solar access to buildings for both passive and active systems, for solar heating, solar control, and day lighting. The solar envelope provides zoning for low-impact development and opens new aesthetic possibilities for both architecture and urban design.

One of the chief objections to solar-access zoning has come from developers concerned with the loss of property rights. But extensive research shows that when achieved by using the solar envelope, solar access does not automatically result in the elimination of tall buildings nor does it mandate suburban densities. Floor-to-area ratios (FARs) as high as 7.5 for mixed-use development and housing densities in excess of 100 dwelling units per acre (du/ac) (247 du/ha) can be achieved.[5] This far exceeds subur-

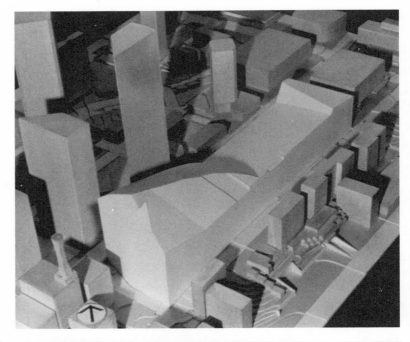

Bunker Hill Project: (Top) The solar envelope, viewed from the south, varies in height from 100 ft to 500 ft (30 m to 152 m); (Bottom) A close-up view of an exemplary design, with floor to area ratio (FAR) of 7.5, trades off some of the development potential of the envelope (FAR = 20) for solar access to buildings and spaces within project boundaries. (Designer: Randall Hong in *Sun Rhythm Form* by Knowles 1981, 268f, 280f.)

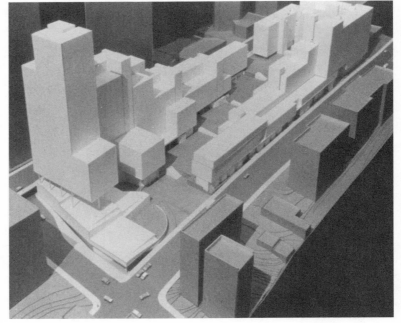

ban densities and would be consistent with the densities of most urban areas in the United States, with the exception of such high-rise centers as Manhattan.

The solar envelope does not abolish tall buildings but rather affects the scale of urban growth. Density can increase over time, according to public values, but violent disruptions of city scale are avoided. Where high-rise development already exists, the solar envelope can be used to protect rooftops and upper-floor solar access. New construction is always shaped and proportioned with reference to the old.

The solar envelope liberates and challenges the architect to design with nature. Because sunshine is assured, designers can make use of the changing directions and properties of light without fear that a taller building will one day cancel their ideas. The potential exists to conceive of architecture in other than static terms of form and space.

Architects can commit to building and urban form in response to orientation. One side of a building will not look like another and one side of a street will not look like another. Development will tend to be lower on the south side of a street than on the north where a major southern exposure is thus preserved. Streets take on a directional character where orientation is clearly recognized. Buildings and streets assume separate identities, providing a basis for what Kevin Lynch called "way finding."[6]

The way shadow fences are set determines the character of streets. When set at all property lines, sides as well as front and back, building façades rise and fall. A design research project that shows this condition within the diagonal Spanish grid of downtown Los Angeles results in densities of 80 to 100 du/ac (198 to 247 du/ha). The envelopes are generated to provide 4 hours of sunshine in winter and 8 hours in summer; they slope downward to a 20-foot (6.1 m) shadow fence at all property lines to accommodate

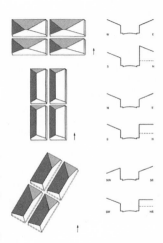

Street orientation changes the solar envelope's form and thus street sections.

Housing Project on the Spanish Grid, Viewed from the East: (Top) The solar envelopes appear crystal-like while existing buildings are rectilinear blocks; (Bottom) Housing designs under the envelope achieve a density range of 80 to 100 du/ac (198 to 247 du/ha) over street-front commercial. (The old Spanish grid runs at about 36 degrees off the north–south axis of the US Land Ordinance of 1785.)

a base of street-front shops under housing. The envelopes are consistently higher on the south than on the north with the exception of towerlike shapes that project upward at some corners where shadows are allowed to extend further northward into streets, but not onto properties across the street.

Housing Project on Curving Streets, Viewed from the South: (Left) Solar envelopes run continuously along the street, dropping to shadow fences only at front and back of lots; (Right) Housing designs under the envelope achieve a density range of 25 to 45 du/ac (62 to 111 du/ha), much higher than normal subdivision densities.

When building designs fill the solar envelopes, they contain many traditional elements. Roof terraces appear where the rectangular geometry of construction meets the sloping envelope. Courtyards center many designs to achieve a proper exposure for sunshine and air. Façades are enriched by porches, screens, and clerestories—all differentiated by orientation to the sun and wind. Beyond the appearance of such time-honored means, adjacent buildings meet each other gently, across sloping spaces, not abruptly across property sidelines and alleys. The resulting spaces, not confining and dark but rather liberating and filled with light, allow distance views and the free flow of air through the city.

When shadow fences are set only at front and back property lines but not at sidelines, solar envelopes run continuously to allow for an unbroken façade along a typical suburban street. A studio project that tests this condition replaces suburban densities of 5 to 7 du/ac (12 to 17 du/ha) with higher densities of 25 to 45 du/ac (62 to 111 du/ha). The solar envelopes rise and fall with changes in street orientation and lot size. Envelope rules provide longer periods of sunshine than in the first project: 6 hours on a winter day, 10 hours in summer. They are generated to a 6-foot (1.8 m) high shadow fence across streets at neighboring front yards and at rear property lines. Since envelopes do not drop at property sidelines as in the first project, buildings are free to run continuously along the street.

When building designs replace the envelopes, the result is remarkable innovation within harmony. The continuous envelopes allow a smooth flow of street fronts. At the same time, building types range from town houses and courtyard clusters to apartments. Individual designers are clearly exploring separate formal ideas from one parcel to another. The consequence, if these were built, would be an enormous range of diversity and choice within a neighborhood.

A Study of Development Potential in Housing

Los Angeles is the location of a rigorous 10-year housing study of the solar envelope's development potential.[7] The study sought to find an alternative to present housing practices, and to illustrate different ways Los Angeles can use the solar envelope in different circumstances. Actual sites were selected for their different land values, topographies, street orientations, and neighborhood characteristics to test the effectiveness of the envelope over a range of conditions. In most cases, the sites already had buildings on them.

Final designs of the study were not built, although test results have occasionally acted as a zoning guide for Los Angeles city planners.

Because of modern development pressures, the study tried for the highest housing densities while assuring solar access to all dwelling units during some part of the day. The research data relate *density* (a count of dwelling units per acre, generally corresponding to land values) to *S:V* (surface-to-volume ratio, an energy-related measure of building form). While some circumstances, such as commercial centers, may call for a different scale depending on community values, this relationship between density and S:V is taken as grounds for concluding that three to seven stories generally represent the best size range for urban housing in Los Angeles. These figures can vary among cities but the underlying suppositions of solar-access policy and design are broadly applicable to places of density everywhere.

Los Angeles zoning provides for a range of housing densities. It zones some open areas for densities of only one house per acre (A2) or less, while in built-up areas with high land values, it assigns densities of 200 du/ac (R5) or higher. Between the extremes of A2 and R5, chosen for the study, lies a range of other classifications that provide planners a way to match growth with community values.

Current zoning provides the urban housing reference for this study. First, the dwelling classifications are the actual ones used in the study. Second, they show in which density range Los Angeles planners officially recognize the greatest variety of housing types. Finally, each part of the range symbolizes not only different dwelling classifications but also a separate grouping of possibilities for designers, developers, and users. To evaluate these possibilities, it is useful first to establish the relationship between a measure of building form (S:V) and density.

S:V is a mathematical ratio between exposed surfaces and

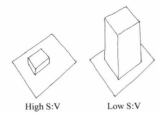

High S:V   Low S:V

contained building volume. For the study, calculations for *surface* include all outside surfaces of the building (all roofs and walls) plus those portions of the site that are exposed. Calculations for *volume* include only the building. A small building on a large lot will have a higher S:V than will a large building on the same size lot.

S:V, measured on the vertical axis of the graph, varies indirectly with building size. Symbols at the highest end of the curve represent small buildings up to three stories on relatively large lots. Symbols at the low, extreme right end of the curve signify large buildings of unlimited height on crowded lots. Between these extremes, in the elbow of the curve, lies an important range of mid-sized buildings, three to seven stories tall, where the greatest possibilities lie for architects to conserve energy while attaining reasonable densities.

S:V acts both as an energy-related descriptor of form and an expression of design choices. The high S:V of a small building on a large lot means that energy must be expended, mainly to overcome surface or "skin" loads and to maintain the lot; but while this is a disadvantage, it also means a favorable architectural connection to sunshine, fresh air, and view because the designer has so many choices to site and configure the building. On the other hand, the low S:V of a very large building crowding its lot means that more energy must be expended to handle the internal stresses of overheating; and while it provides the advantages of higher densities, it also means less potential for the architect to design with nature.

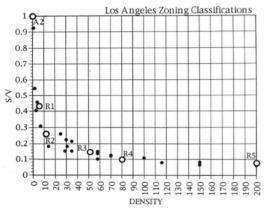

The graph shows the relationship between S:V and density for all Los Angeles housing classifications from 1 to 200 du/ac (2.5 to 494 du/ha). (A few of the more commonly used classifications, as for example R1 for a detached house and R2 for row housing, are marked with a circle.)

Calculations for surface include exposed portions of the lot as well as the building's faces; this combination is used for three reasons. First, zoning codes usually list minimum yard and lot sizes

together with building dimensions as a combined basis for classification. Second, energy is expended to maintain the lot as well as
the building, and when the lot is an acre or more, the proportion
used for lawns and gardens can be enormous. Finally, when assuring solar access for winter heating and access to summer winds for
cooling, the lot and the building must be seen as an integral set.

Density (du/ac), measured on the horizontal axis of the graph,
varies with housing classification. One-family dwellings tend to
have their own yards. Also, one-family houses tend to have more
floor space than a unit within an apartment building.

Density, an indicator of land values, expresses development
options. High densities correspond with inflated land values;
units, and even whole buildings, become compact and essentially
repetitive. Low densities coincide with smaller land costs; developers concentrate on one-family houses multiplied over enormous
tracts. But for urban housing on restricted sites in Los Angeles,
developers usually try for the highest densities the market and
zoning will support. The question is how to balance development
pressures with solar access.

Exemplary Housing Designs

Four housing designs, covering a range of settings and densities,
are shown as examples of the larger study. Each design respects
the solar envelope over its own site, thereby guaranteeing sunshine to its neighbors. The program for each design, within its own
envelope, calls for sunshine and cross-ventilation to all dwelling
units, regardless of type or size, house or apartment. The solar
envelopes are systematically adjusted to increase density in successive projects. A corresponding drop of S:V accurately reflects
both higher densities and an increasing difficulty in achieving
solar access and cross-ventilation to individual units.

Project One. Low density hillside housing with a density range of 7 to 18 du/ac (17 to 44 du/ha): (Top) View from the southwest along the north–south ridge; (Bottom) A close view of housing on the west-facing slope.

Project One

The first project is located on the north–south ridge of a low hill. The program calls for increasing density in an older neighborhood of single-family houses (5 to 7 du/ac; 12 to 17 du/ha). By putting more than one house on an existing lot, projects achieve a density range of 7 to 18 du/ac (17 to 44 du/ha). Individual houses are in the two- to four-bedroom range or about 1350 to 2500 sq ft (125 to 232 sq m).

The solar envelopes guarantee 6 hours of sunshine on a winter day and 10 hours in summer for outdoor recreation and for gardening. Shadowing is allowed at any time below 8 feet (2.4 m) at front and rear property lines but is unlimited at side property lines and on all public rights-of-way.

House designs show great architectural variety. Partly this results from different site conditions, sloping or flat, that affect the solar envelopes. But even within a parcel, relatively high values of S:V provide especially rich possibilities to explore architectural responses to sunlight. Designs generally have more windows on the south to capture the winter sun and fewer on the north, partly to avoid heat loss and also for privacy from next-door neighbors. South-facing clerestories allow the penetration of winter sun down stairways to enliven otherwise darker, lower floors.

Project Two

A second project, planned under identical rules, is located nearby on the eastern slope of the same hill. Here, because the hill flattens, solar envelopes can rise, providing more volume than in the first project. This nearly doubles the density of the first project to 14 to 28 du/ac (34 to 69 du/ha).

House designs on the steeper part of the site show characteristics similar to those seen earlier on the west side of the hill. The solar envelope clearly accentuates the downward tilt of the natural topography. Clerestories over stairwells capture south sun for daylighting and especially for winter heating.

In contrast, houses on a flatter portion of the site become taller where the solar envelope is less restrictive of their shapes. Three-story row houses line up along a very deep lot with small, private gardens and entry along one edge. A very tall, south-facing clere-

Project Two. Lower mid-density housing with a density range of 14 to 28 du/ac (34.5 to 69 du/ha): (Top) View from the south along east-facing slope; (Bottom) View from the south-west on flat portion of site.

story centers each house, providing light and air to an atrium or inside garden. Here, seasonal rhythms are accentuated: sunlight reaches high on the north side in winter and moves downward and finally disappears from the floor in summer, enlivening the adjoining balconied spaces.

This second project shows somewhat less architectural variety

Project Three. Upper mid-density housing with a density range of 38 to 72 du/ac (94 to 178 du/ha): (Top) Overview from the southwest showing tree-lined, central street; (Bottom) A detail view from the northwest showing typical existing housing in near foreground.

than was seen in the first. Windows tend to be more of a single size and shape. Terraces and gardens are smaller and less visible. This is not the result of less desire on the designer's part for creative self-expression, but is almost entirely the result of lowered S:V that lessens possibilities for identifying separate dwelling units.

Project Three

Located on the diagonal Spanish grid near downtown Los Angeles, this project increases densities still higher to a range of 38 to 72 du/ac (94 to 178 du/ha). The program calls for replacing dilapidated one-family dwellings, but not existing multiple-family dwellings, with a market mix of apartment units averaging 1000 sq ft (93 sq m). Parking is below grade on some lots but is naturally ventilated.

Rules for solar envelopes on this site set less generous time and space constraints, thus allowing more volume here than for the first two projects. While the earlier protocol guaranteed 6 hours of direct winter sunshine, the rules here guarantee only 4 hours—the minimum generally recommended for passive design in this "Mediterranean" climate. Shadowing is allowed at any time below 10 feet (3 m) on residences, including existing apartment houses, and below 20 feet (6 m) on commercial properties where they touch the study site. The new designs not only do not overshadow the older buildings; they are scaled sympathetically to them.

Older buildings on the site follow standard building-line zoning that produces a monotonous regularity of cubical shapes. Within each building, there is a lack of variety of apartment types. In addition, the buildings are spaced so close together that individual apartments often lack air, light, and view.

By comparison, proposed designs under the diversified solar envelopes show more richness of form. The result is not only a variety of building sizes and shapes but also a mixture of apartment types within each building. The consequence is greater choice than is offered by standard development practice. Also, each apartment in the new designs has exposure to light, air, and view.

Western European apartment prototypes have been adapted to solve the problem of solar access and cross-ventilation in this project. Higher densities in the United States generally depend on "double-loaded" corridors and mechanical systems. But in these European designs, hallways systematically skip some floors, allowing units to pass freely both over and under for access to light and air in opposite directions.

When these model sections are applied under actual site conditions, adjustments are usually made at the top and bottom. For example, because cross-ventilation can be achieved through the roof and one side as well as through opposing or adjacent sides, top units can be double loaded on a corridor. And the ground floor can be adapted either as townhouses or as shops facing a street. Adjustments of this sort appear regularly in Projects Three and Four.

Orientation sets the depth of these sections. A building depth of 40 to 45 feet (12.2 to 13.7 m) is about right for north–south exposures, whereas the depth for an east–west exposure averages 50 to 55 feet (15.2 to 16.8 m). This results from the fact that useful sunlight, especially in winter, can only enter from one side of a north–south section. But light enters from two sides of an east–west section: 2 to 3 hours from the east in morning, another 2 to 3 hours from the west in the afternoon, thus enlivening most of the space in the deeper unit.

Two different ways of facing units to the sun profoundly affect the rhythms of experience, and very likely the habits, of life. People occupying an east–west-facing unit are mainly aware of a diurnal rhythm. Early morning light reaches far inside east-facing rooms, then gradually recedes throughout the morning. Afternoon light first enters west-facing rooms in early afternoon and then gradually spreads inward until sunset. Where someone chooses to read the newspaper, take a nap, or work on a computer can vary over the day.

By contrast, people in north–south-facing units are more likely

Housing sections developed in western Europe: Best for east–west exposures, (a) by Dutch architect Jacob Bakema and (b) by French architect Le Corbusier; sections (c) and (d) adapted in the University of Southern California Solar Studio for north–south exposures.

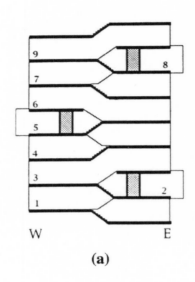

(a)

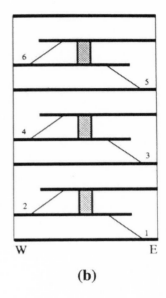

(b)

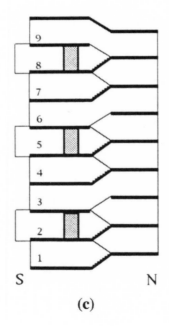

(c)

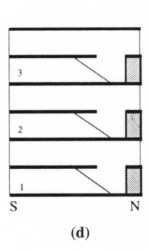

(d)

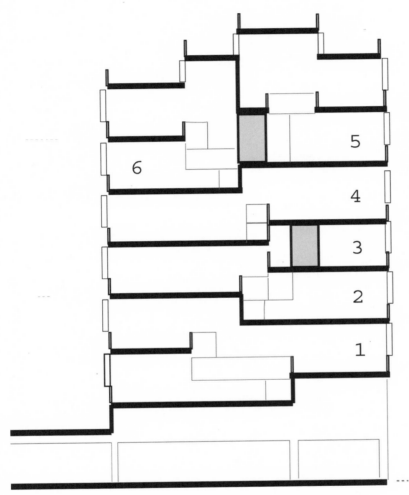

Modified Bakema Housing
Section: Double-loaded top
corridor where exposed roofs,
in addition to walls, provide
light and cross-ventilation;
Townhouses or shops
on the ground floor.

Project Four. High-density housing with a density range of 76 to 128 du/ac (188 to 316 du/ha): (Top) A view from the southeast showing three separate designs in the foreground sharing a continuous envelope that intentionally overshadows a public park; (Bottom) A view from the northwest showing two well-integrated designs in the foreground, again sharing a continuous envelope.

to be aware of the passing seasons. Midwinter light will reach deep inside those rooms facing south, even to the back walls and perhaps beyond, into a next adjoining layer of space. Midsummer light will likely not enter the south rooms at all but will angle shallowly into north-facing rooms very early in the morning and again late in the afternoon before sunset. Under these circumstances, the relative location of bedrooms or living rooms can make a big difference to life in the place.

Project Four

Located on a hillside close to downtown, this project achieves a density range of 76 to 128 du/ac (188 to 316 du/ha), the highest densities reached in the study. The site is inappropriate for very large commercial structures but ideal for the high-density housing that is so needed in the downtown area. Design requirements for unit size and parking are the same as for the third project, and the building sections diagrammed there are used here as well.

Solar-envelope rules for time constraints are the same as for the third project, but the space constraints have been altered. First, there are no sideline setbacks. Second, the solar envelope runs continuously without dropping at property sidelines. Finally, overshadowing is purposely allowed on a north-facing slope that has been left open as a public park. Combined, these three changes have the effect of providing more envelope volume than in any of the earlier projects. S:V also drops to the lowest value achieved in the study, setting a limit on density while still providing solar access and cross-ventilation to every housing unit.

Research Findings

These four housing projects cover a density range that falls short of the full range of densities possible under Los Angeles zoning, but for two different and opposing reasons. The lowest housing density of the study, 7 du/ac (17 du/ha), was deliberate, an initial decision to exclude from investigation one-family dwellings on very big lots as inappropriate for urban housing. On the other hand, the high end of the range, 128 du/ac (316 du/ha), was not deliberate but the result of the design and envelope rules systematically set for each of the four projects. This density range embraces a remarkable variety of ways to live in the city within a height range of three to seven stories. Ample opportunities exist in this midsize range to provide both energy conservation and a better quality of life without constricting development options for urban growth.

Graph of Study Results:
All 150 designs fall within the elbow of the curve, covering a density range of 7 to 128 du/ac (17 to 316 du/ha).

The single most important discovery of the study is represented on the graph by the clustering of symbols in the elbow of the curve. This clustering represents a critical lower cutoff value of S:V=0.1, which corresponds with a maximum density of about 100 du/ac (247 du/ha). A few special conditions, such as a park or wide boulevard where longer shadows could be cast without harming a neighboring property, resulted in taller buildings with fractionally lower S:V values. Otherwise, for good solar access and cross-ventilation in a compact and continuous urban fabric, the rule holds. Designers who break this rule lose the choice of architectural means to sustain building comfort and must depend on energy-intensive systems.

So far, the solar envelope has been described as a fixed boundary on development. There is, however, a dynamic potential of the solar envelope that offers a new promise for architecture. The solar envelope can do more than guarantee solar access; it can open design options for major building transformations.

Because of the seasonally shifting earth–sun geometry, the solar envelope can expand its boundaries in summer and contract them in winter without overshadowing neighbors. Between the summer and winter envelopes, there is an interstitial space where flexible structures can expand and contract with the seasons as a means of adapting to program and climate change. This *interstitium* thus creates the potential for architecture to recapture a time-rich basis for the ritual use of space.

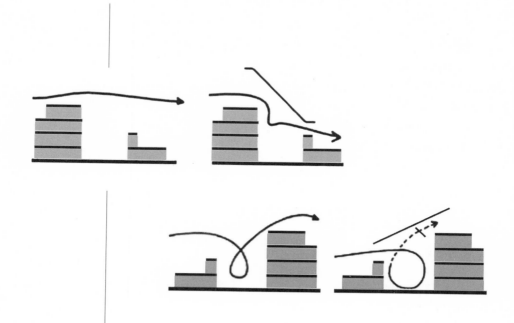

9 | The Interstitium

W ORKS THAT ARE DYNAMIC AND BASED ON SYSTEMS IN these times of dynamism and systems . . . invite our participation in their lives." Thus, architect Eduardo Catalano speaks of a great mechanical flower, *Floralis Generica*, that he designed for the Plaza Naciones Unidas in Buenos Aires.[1] The flower, based on the hibiscus, opens and closes giant petals with the days and seasons ". . . to integrate the creations of man with the creations of the earth." The work is now a popular reality in a civic space where people of all ages gather around and are reminded of their connection to nature.

Catalano's flower, by opening and closing daily, symbolizes a new vision for architecture. Traditional modes of sheltering corresponded with nature's rhythms and, at the same time, evoked rich patterns of social behavior. A dynamic interpretation of solar-envelope zoning can advance the integration of such traditional methods and, at the same time, support the dynamism of a new architectural paradigm—one based on a dialogue with nature that will give architecture its identity.

The solar envelope has been earlier defined as the largest theoretical volume on a building site that does not critically overshadow neighbors, but the size and shape of the envelope need not be fixed. It may contract in winter and expand in summer while still allowing the same period of solar access to adjacent properties. Between the winter envelope and the generally higher summer envelope is an intervening space, a region of temporality that can accommodate seasonal adjustments to program and climate. Analogies drawn from nature have provided a name for this region: *interstitium.*

The term "interstitium" is borrowed from human anatomy. The interstitial space of the lung is that area of tissue between the

Terraced Buildings: Designed under solar envelopes by architecture students.

alveoli (tiny air sacs) and the capillaries that carry the blood. When we breathe in, the alveoli expand with air, and the interstitium stretches into a very thin layer. In this way, alveoli and capillaries are brought into close proximity so the oxygen has less distance to travel in its diffusion from outer world (alveolus) to inner world (capillary). When we breathe out, the process reverses and the interstitium contracts. Like Catalano's flower, architecture can also expand and contract in response to the cycles of nature.

We have seen that the basic solar envelope, generally derived from winter sun angles, tends to produce roof terraces, a real benefit for urban living. When the right angles of most building construction meet the sloping geometry of the solar envelope, stepped roofs are a natural result. Instead of abandoning these terraces as left-out roofs, they can be designed spaces for enriching urban life. They can also replace the ground level covered by the building: "green roofs" for gardening, growing fruits, vegetables and flowers, and small trees—absorbing carbon dioxide and releasing oxygen into the atmosphere, attracting birds, bees, and butterflies. But municipalities that limit the building envelope by applying only winter sun angles preclude some important dynamic possibilities for design.

An architectural interstitium, by rising above the basic envelope, expands possibilities for responding to changing seasons. A building might, for many good reasons, transform from a tighter, compact winter mode to a looser arrangement in summer. Flexible structures, comprising either the whole or some part of a building, might expand and contract, making use of different seasonal envelopes. And all surrounding properties can enjoy these same design choices as well.

The functional needs of buildings quite often change with the seasons.[2] This sort of cyclic behavior may include advertising, selling, entertaining, manufacturing, sports, and gardening. Some changes can be accommodated within the fixed boundaries of the basic envelope. Others, as for example temporary housing for summer tourists or a theater under the warm nighttime sky, can benefit from a flexible structure. Summer cafés, market fairs, art exhibits, and expanded common rooms for apartment dwellers are other possible uses.

The interstitium provides the space for adding open trellises, lattice structures for supporting deciduous plants and vines that shed their leaves in winter, gaining them back in spring for summer shade. It even allows for

Interstitium on Diagonally Oriented Site: Each of three overlapping seasonal envelopes (winter solstice, equinox, and summer solstice) provides the same 6 hours of solar access to surrounding properties. Between the low winter and high summer envelopes is a dynamic interstitial space allowing buildings to change.

Functional Changes: (Left) Winter and summer envelopes; (Middle) Diagrammatic building—winter mode; (Right) Diagrammatic theater and marquee—summer mode. (Computer drawings by Karen Kensek in "The Interstitium: A zoning strategy for seasonally adaptive architecture" by Knowles and Kensek 2000; 774. In K. Steemers and S. Yannas, eds., *Proceedings of PLEA 2000: Architecture, City, Environment*.)

the summertime addition of folding rooms, screened for warm-weather sleeping or recreation. When combined with roof gardens, the result is an important enrichment of urban life.

In the illustration of functional changes, the low winter and higher summer envelopes are each designed to provide 6 hours (9 a.m.–3 p.m.) of direct sunshine to neighbors. The winter envelope has a complex shape, but a single plane dominates the higher summer envelope. The difference of shape results from shifting sun angles. Low winter rays from the sun approach the site from the southeast at 9 a.m. and from the southwest at 3 p.m. By contrast, higher summer rays come in from nearly due east at 9 a.m. and due west at 3 p.m. When shadow fences follow the rectangular grid of the 1785 US Land Ordinance, the useful portion of the summer envelope is, for the most part, a single plane.

The interstitium, besides accommodating the flexible use of space, can act as a shield, a zone of defense against climatic extremes. Shading devices that rise during the summer months for comfort in outdoor spaces or to cool the roof and reduce air-conditioning loads can come down in winter. In some climates, such as Hawaii, rain catchers might rise for protection from downpours and to catch precious fresh water. Such shields might be as small as a parasol or as large as a circus tent, operated manually or completely automated with a kinetic device responding to sun, wind, or water.

Ventilation stacks can rise above the winter roofline allowing

Climatic Adaptations:
(Left) Winter and
summer envelopes;
(Middle) Diagrammatic
building—winter mode;
(Right) Diagrammatic
ventilation stacks and
courtyard cover—summer
mode. (Computer drawings
by Karen Kensek in "The
Interstitium: A zoning
strategy for seasonally
adaptive architecture" by
Knowles and Kensek 2000;
774. In K. Steemers and
S. Yannas, eds., *Proceedings
of PLEA 2000: Architecture,
City, Environment*.)

for interior heat to be vented in summer. Structures resembling large awnings or umbrellas can shade and ventilate the courtyard. Hence, the summer landscape might unfold with clusters of diamond-shaped sails or kites floating motionless and weightless above the rooftops. The winter landscape might collapse inward, appearing lower and smoother than in summer. All such means are expansions of ways people have traditionally achieved comfort while conserving energy.

Large deciduous trees, valued for both climate control and beauty, can be accommodated by the interstitium. Studies have shown a summertime difference of as much as 42°F (23°C) in urban surface temperatures between those well shaded by trees and those in direct sun. Unfortunately, conventional solar-access zoning can work against trees. Clearly, evergreens do need to be limited to the winter envelope to avoid harmful overshadowing of neighboring properties. Otherwise, for trees that lose their leaves in winter, there is no reason why they shouldn't rise in maturity to fill summer boundaries of the interstitium.

Courtyards and the Interstitium

Courtyard buildings, because they are so common throughout the world, deserve special attention for the advantages they offer as an urban type. In making a strong supporting argument for the courtyard, architect John Reynolds has described its many traditional uses. "Courtyards serve buildings of nearly every imaginable function. Residences are [often] . . . designed around courtyards, because courtyards offer both privacy and access to nature. Commercial activities also benefit. For example, restaurants offer shaded courtyards as escapes from oppressive small offices and the midday heat. Hotels use flowering courtyards as the first impression for their guests, and the surrounding arcades for lobby functions."[3]

Using the interstitial space of the solar envelope can expand the potential of courtyards, offering architects a powerful tool for designing in cities. With so many possible functions and endless variations of size and shape, there are numerous ways to make courtyards serve as dynamic spatial intersections, domains of choice that are both culturally and climatically responsive.

Building on the example of the Spanish toldo, modern ways can be found to achieve comfort in courtyards. Reynolds points out that, as traditionally applied in Spain, the toldo nearly fills the sky opening of the courtyard, interfering with ventilation.[4] It might thus be seen as disadvantageous despite its obvious advantage for shade. However, by taking advantage of the interstitium, a courtyard cover can rise above the building to shield from summer sun and, at the same time, to direct cooling winds downward to the patio floor. In winter, the cover withdraws so that the courtyard can receive sunshine and less direct wind.

Los Angeles, like Spain, has a long history of courtyard buildings. The era of courtyard buildings in Los Angeles dates from the 18th century Spanish missions to elegant housing of the 1920s. Then the building boom after World War II mostly rejected this history in favor of air-conditioned tract houses and high-rises. Now, concerns for earthquake safety and for energy conservation, as well as the need for greater density, have awakened interest in midrise courtyard buildings for many different applications.

The climate of Los Angeles is sometimes described as Mediterranean. Rainfall is light and seasonal, coming mostly in late fall and early winter. Seasonal temperature transitions are modest. Summers are warm, requiring light clothing, but are rarely uncomfortably hot, especially if one can find some shade. Winters are cool but almost never freezing and, in the sunshine, can be quite pleasant. At all seasons, daily temperature changes average about 20°F (11.2°C), a very useful difference for "flushing" the house at night before the next daily cycle of heating.

To achieve year-round comfort in Los Angeles courtyards, the traditional modes of migration and transformation are useful adaptive strategies. People can move daily seeking either sun or shadow, engaging the entire space. Toldo-like structures can rise and fall, changing space completely with the seasons. But how and when these time-honored strategies come into play depend on the site and its surroundings.

The circumstances of sun and wind that provide comfort in Los Angeles courtyards vary seasonally. Prevailing winds from the west are desirable for summer ventilation and cooling. Winter sun in the courtyard is desirable while summer sun is not. Orientation of a courtyard makes a big difference for the entry of both sun and wind.

COURTYARDS ELONGATED NORTH TO SOUTH

Daily changes of light and shadow are the most persistent influence when the courtyard is elongated north and south. There are, of course, seasonal changes as well but as in the Gothic transept or a north–south running street, it is the daily rhythm that is most intensely felt. The longer courtyard walls on the east and west cast the bigger shadows and are the overriding influence on where people are likely to stroll or to sit.

The diagrammatic example shows simple courtyard walls of equal height on all sides, but massing will affect courtyard

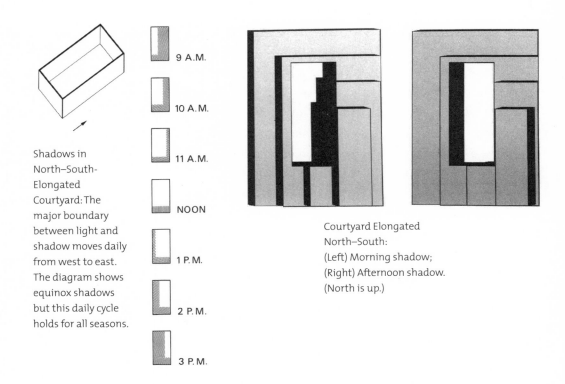

Shadows in North–South-Elongated Courtyard: The major boundary between light and shadow moves daily from west to east. The diagram shows equinox shadows but this daily cycle holds for all seasons.

9 A.M.

10 A.M.

11 A.M.

NOON

1 P.M.

2 P.M.

3 P.M.

Courtyard Elongated North–South:
(Left) Morning shadow;
(Right) Afternoon shadow.
(North is up.)

shadows. Height and shape of the surrounding mass of the building, along with courtyard proportions, work together to affect shadows. Regardless of such differences, daily rhythms remain predominant.

Open courtyards in this orientation receive full midday summer sun; fortunately, unless they are excessively deep, they also get a fair portion of the midday winter sun. The Los Angeles winter sun rises to the south of east and sets to the south of west, attaining a low-altitude angle due south at noon. Still, winter shadows do not reach the north end of the patio for a considerable period of the midday, leaving a sunny place where office workers may want to relax in the garden for socializing during their lunch break.

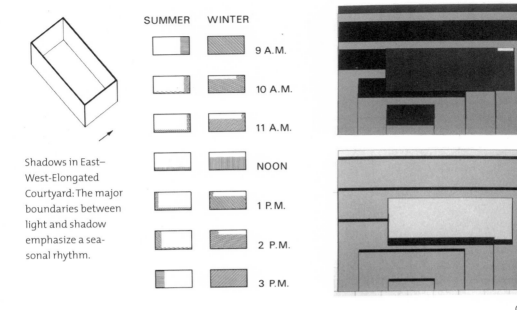

SUMMER | WINTER
9 A.M.
10 A.M.
11 A.M.
NOON
1 P.M.
2 P.M.
3 P.M.

Shadows in East–West-Elongated Courtyard: The major boundaries between light and shadow emphasize a seasonal rhythm.

Courtyards Elongated East–West: (Top) Midday, winter, the patio is completely in shadow; (Bottom) Midday, summer, the patio is nearly all in direct sun and requires protection. (North is up.)

COURTYARDS ELONGATED EAST TO WEST

A seasonal cycle of light and shadow, and more especially of heat and cold, structures life within east–west-elongated courtyards. There are daily changes as well. But it is the seasons that are most intensely felt because of the dominating effect of deep shadows cast by the long wall on the south edge of the courtyard.

Again, the diagrammatic example shows a simple courtyard. Massing will affect courtyard shadows here as well. But even when the massing is more complex, the basic rhythm of change remains seasonal.

In Los Angeles, with prevailing summer winds from the west and winter sun from the south, a courtyard orientation that works with the sun can work against the wind and vice versa. This is an especially critical factor in designing a courtyard cover if the space beneath it is to be a garden where people habitually go to relax or even to spend some part of their working day outside their offices.

Contradictions between sun and wind in courtyards of either orientation are resolved by using the interstitium. Adjustable structures can expand upward during hot summer months, catching ocean breezes from the west and simultaneously shading the courtyard. During winter, when the sun is lower and there is less need for ventilation in the courtyard, the cover withdraws, opening the courtyard again to the sky. In most cases, by providing ample space for such a structure to float freely, the interstitium offers a way to give year-round comfort by low-energy means. But orientation and surroundings make all the difference.

Comparing Four Site Orientations

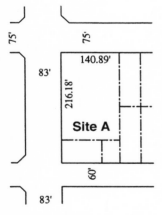

Site A: Actual Los Angeles site in mixed-use neighborhood. (North is up.)

An actual Los Angeles site in a mixed-use neighborhood provides a range of conditions to demonstrate how migration and transformation can provide comfort in courtyards. The site, a corner lot measuring 141 by 216 feet (43 by 66 m) is bounded on two sides by streets and on the opposing two sides by adjacent mixed-use properties. A proposed office building for the site has an elongated courtyard measuring 47 by 122 feet (14.3 by 37.2 m). Depending on overall building dimensions, a perimeter of usable office space approximately 50 feet deep (15.2 m) surrounds the courtyard. Streets and lots are oriented on the cardinal points following the US Land Ordinance of 1785.

Envelope rules include shadow fences of 20 feet (6 m) at commercial properties across streets to north and west of the site, and 10 feet (3 m) on adjacent mixed-use lots to the east and south. Cutoff times for the envelope provide neighboring properties with 6 hours of direct sunshine, 9 a.m. to 3 p.m., at all seasons. Those same cutoff times will produce a much higher envelope in summer than in winter, thus defining the interstitium.

The winter envelope is the main reference for the fixed building mass and for the up-and-down interstitium. A courtyard building that follows this winter envelope is high on the west and north, lower on the east and south. The interstitium, bounded on top by a much higher envelope, slopes as a single imaginary plane following the different sun geometry of summer. Within this space between the building and the higher plane of the summer envelope is the interstitium that accommodates the seasonal courtyard cover.

A more complete understanding of the importance of orientation comes from imagining the actual site (Site A) systematically rotated on the cardinal points. With each rotation, adjacent conditions change, altering the direction and distance that shadows can be cast off site and thus the envelope's size and shape. Changed too is the courtyard orientation, affecting how and when sun and wind can enter.

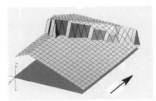

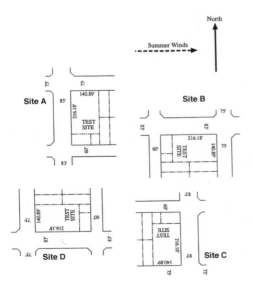

Rotation of Site A: Starting on the upper left and moving clockwise. (North is up.)

Site A: (Top) Winter solar envelope; (2nd from top) Building mass to maximize space of winter envelope; (3rd from top) Summer envelope defines upper limit of interstitium; (Bottom) Adjustable courtyard cover. (Viewed from the southeast.)

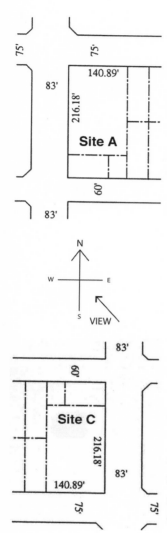

North–South-Elongated Sites:
(Top) Actual corner site
A in Los Angeles;
(Bottom) Site C, rotated 180
degrees from site A.

While the setting effectively changes with each site rotation, certain design conditions are fixed. The rules for solar envelope generation remain constant, but the space inside the envelopes changes dramatically. Regardless of the size or shape of the envelopes, several conditions applying to the resulting buildings remain unchanged. Each building maximizes the space of its corresponding solar envelope at a floor-to-floor height of 14 feet (4.3 m). Walls are designed with no wind openings; they are closed at the street level to increase shop frontage and to avoid street dust and noise. Windows at the upper levels are presumed to be a hit or miss proposition and not reliable for ventilating the courtyard. All useful airflow occurs only through the courtyard opening.

COMPARISON OF SITES A AND C

Sites A and C both run long in the north–south direction but different arrangements of surrounding properties alter envelope outlines. Generally, where streets touch the site, envelopes rise; where mixed-use properties touch, envelopes drop.

In any courtyard elongated in a north–south direction, people will generally find continuous choices for comfort just by crossing shadow boundaries, the direction and distance of movement corresponding with different rhythms. Seasonally, they will usually find comfort by shifting northward in winter and southward in summer. Daily, they will follow a broad boundary moving from west to east. Only between 9 a.m. and 3 p.m. in summer is the courtyard likely to be uncomfortably flooded with sunshine. That 6-hour period sets the condition for designing a courtyard cover. Otherwise there is a dilemma: to be in the hot sun or to stay out of the courtyard completely.

While open courtyards in this orientation provide ample choices of sunlight and shadow most of the year, they can deny wind for ventilation. This may be an advantage in winter but on a

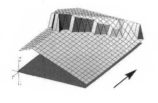

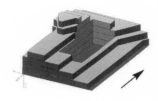

Solar Envelopes:
(Top) Envelope A;
(Bottom) Envelope C.
(Viewed from the southeast.)

Building Masses:
(Top) Building A;
(Bottom) Building C.

hot summer day, cooling breezes from the Pacific Ocean pass over the building, leaving the courtyard hot and still.

Envelope rules for both sites are the same but directions of adjoining streets and properties are different, thus affecting the size and shape of the envelope. Envelope A is high on the north and west where shadows can be cast across streets to meet 20-foot shadow fences at commercial properties. Envelope C, on the other hand, is high on the south and east for the same reason. Understanding the difference is basic to designing for sun and wind.

The two buildings admit sunlight differently into their own courtyards. Because building A is high on the west, winter sun enters the courtyard throughout the morning and midday but not in the afternoon, discouraging winter afternoon use. In contrast, building C favors winter afternoon use; its high mass on the east and south blocks winter morning sun, but sunlight floods the courtyard throughout the midday and afternoon.

Summer envelopes, defining the upper boundaries of the interstitium, slope in different directions on the two sites. The envelope for site A slopes down to the east and is determined by afternoon rays of the summer sun. In contrast, the envelope for site C slopes down to the west following rays of the morning sun. The

High Summer Envelopes
Bound Interstitial Space:
(Top) Interstitium A;
(Bottom) Interstitium C.

Courtyard Covers:
(Top) Cover A;
(Bottom) Cover C.

contrast sets different limits on courtyard covers that must remain inside the interstitial space between the building mass and the summer envelope.

Courtyard covers, designed to control both sun and wind in the courtyards, stay within the interstitium to avoid overshadowing neighbors in summer. Cover A is in two parts, high on the west to capture wind and shaped to accommodate variations in wall height. Cover C is low on the west, rising above the building-mass and is shaped on its leeward edge to protect stepping walls from direct sun. In both cases, the covers successfully meet shading requirements, but ventilation of their courtyards is a different matter altogether.

Courtyard covers, in addition to protecting from summer sun, are designed to channel wind gently downward to people on the patio floor. Courtyard A is the more difficult to solve for ventilation. Without a cover, there is little or no air movement inside the courtyard. High building-mass on the west forces wind up and over the building. Even with the cover in place, there is still no air movement at the patio level. In contrast, the lower mass on the windward side of building C improves the chance for good ventilation. Without the cover, breezes barely reach the patio floor. But

with the cover in place, ventilation is good to excellent. Beyond that advantage derived from massing, cover C is designed with a baffle that further enhances ventilation.

COMPARISON OF SITES B AND D

Sites B and D are both elongated east to west. Courtyards will also run east and west. Site B has streets on the north and east while site D has them on the south and west.

It is important to note that illustrations for B and D use a different viewpoint from A and C. Illustrations for A and C showed views from the southeast, so that north in the pictures generally conformed to the orientation of site plans. However, to better understand building massing and courtyard-cover shapes for sites B and D, the viewpoint for illustrations has been shifted to the northwest. (Note view arrow on site plans.)

As in the previous two cases, the covering envelopes are different. Both are high on the south and low on the north. But envelope B provides more potential building volume because shadows can extend across the street on the north.

Both resulting buildings have greater mass on the south than on the north but building B is taller with more floors resulting in more extreme courtyard conditions: deep winter shade and hot summer sun. Building D has similar sun conditions but not so extreme because the building is not so tall and the courtyard is more open to ambient light from the sky. In both cases, the cover provides summer protection for the courtyard but the lack of winter sun cannot be solved without a design change in the building mass.

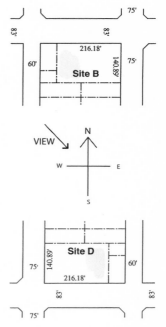

East–West-Elongated Sites:
(Top) Site B;
(Bottom) Site D, rotated
180 degrees from site B.

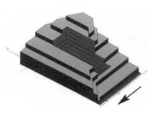

Solar Envelopes:
(Top) Envelope B;
(Bottom) Envelope D.
(While north is up in
the site plans, the images
here are viewed from the
northwest.)

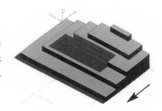

Building Masses:
(Top) Building B;
(Bottom) Building D.

While neither courtyard performs well for sunshine, both do much better for ventilation. Still, there is a difference between the two. The courtyard wall of building B is lower on the west end than on the east, effectively channeling summer breezes from the ocean. Building D has the opposite condition, higher on the west than on the east, but since the building is generally lower with fewer stories, ventilation of the open courtyard is moderately good.

Summer envelopes, each defining the upper boundary of its interstitium, peak midway along the two sites. The major plane for envelope B slopes down to the west and is determined by morning rays of the summer sun; a minor plane is less critical. The major plane for envelope D slopes down to the east following rays of the afternoon sun, but, in this instance, a minor plane is also important.

With courtyard covers in place, ventilation is excellent. Cover B is in two parts, but wind enters only at the lower level since it cannot simultaneously enter at both windward openings. The wind then exits at the upper windward level and to the side (dotted). Cover D is simpler, one piece rising high to catch the westerly winds.

RITUAL HOUSE

Summer Envelopes Defining
Upper Boundary of Interstitium:
(Top) Interstitium B;
(Bottom) Interstitium D.

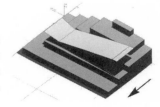

Courtyard Covers Designed
within Interstitium:
(Top) Cover B;
(Bottom) Cover D.

In each of the four examples, the courtyard covers are unique, and they satisfy in different ways the summer conditions of sun and wind. The requirements for summer shading are completely met. The requirements for ventilation are also met, but with varying degrees of success. The configurations shown for courtyard covers represent only one set of design possibilities. Alternatives, perhaps better ones, are surely possible.

Such large structures that expand upward into the interstitium would very likely need to be mechanized. Perhaps if the application is small, as in a house, adjustments can be manual as with the

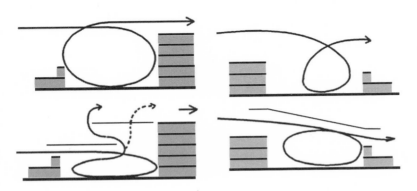

Sections Showing
Wind Flow over Open
and Covered Courts:
(Left) Site B;
(Right) Site D.

Spanish toldo. But at a scale to match a midrise office building or multiple housing, the courtyard cover would doubtless require electrical motors and gears that need not operate especially fast and that can be efficient to run.

Courtyard covers might vary dramatically in opacity, texture, color, and construction. For example, they might be translucent as the Spanish toldo or striped as some Bedouin tents, smooth as a circus tent or textured as a veil, white or tinted. They might move as a whole piece on a collapsible frame or in sections pulled along spanning wires. All such differences of design would tell a more complete story of a place than just a simple outline.

The four designs illustrate renewed possibilities for a ritual courtyard life corresponding with natural rhythms. This is true for buildings in general, but perhaps it is especially so for commercial offices where workers spend so much of their time in cities. Office buildings have generally been designed to keep workers at their desks, but laptop computers and cell phones now make it possible to move around. There is no reason why workers can't just as well do at least some of their work in a courtyard garden with flowers and trees, with the sounds of birds and water, and with winter sun to warm them and summer shade and breezes to cool them. Why not offer a choice of working inside or out, at a desk or on a garden bench? The change of surroundings can make people more, not less productive. Clearly, different climates suggest alternative approaches but why deny the option where the setting makes it possible?

Flexible architecture can deepen the experience of seasons and enrich social patterns, but orientation makes a difference. People can at all seasons enjoy courtyards elongated north and south. Winter draws sharp contrasts under the open sky: garden fountains, streams, and pools glisten; hands, arms, and faces are warmed in the bright sun. In summer, the details of winter lose their sharpness under filtered light. In either season, people enjoy access to nature in an expanded common room, a regular release from small offices.

On the other hand, people are more likely to avoid winter conditions in a courtyard that is elongated east and west. Even in the Mediterranean climate of Los Angeles, office workers may regularly come forth only when the cover is again raised for ventilation and shading: late spring, summer, and early fall. (One unexplored option to rectify this undesirable condition would be to remove some building mass on the south.) Furthermore, the courtyard example is only one instance of a dynamic architectural adjustment under the interstitium. The challenge to designers is to conceive of others.

Looking to the Future

The benefits of solar-access zoning can be realized around the world. The results of the Los Angeles studies, done at 34°N, can apply directly to any city at approximately the same latitude either north or south of the equator. Some of these are Baghdad, Tehran, Kabul, Lahore, Osaka, Tokyo, Buenos Aires, and Santiago. For cities at other latitudes, the size and shape of the solar envelope will vary, but the basic principles hold.

Investigations of the solar envelope have also been done in places at latitudes other than 34°N. The most northerly location is Bratislava at 48°N, where a mixed-use study was made in 1993 at the Slovak Technical University. The most southerly site is Honolulu at 21°N where, between 1999 and 2000, two separate hillside-housing studies were made at the University of Hawaii at Manoa. Design and development requirements were met in each case, confirming the value of solar-access zoning within a broad belt from at least 50°N to 50°S.

Tests of Solar Envelope: Confirming that the solar envelope is practical for most of the world.

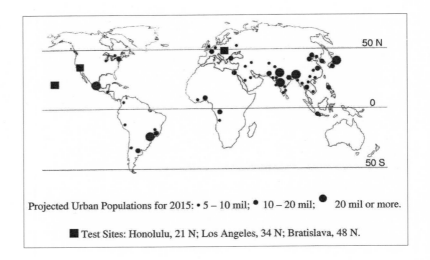

Projected Urban Populations for 2015: • 5 – 10 mil; ● 10 – 20 mil; ● 20 mil or more.

■ Test Sites: Honolulu, 21 N; Los Angeles, 34 N; Bratislava, 48 N.

In many places, architects who are interested in energy conservation are already working with dynamic systems that can vividly change the aspect of a building.[5] Some are using such mechanized devices as outside sunscreens that are programmed to rotate on a vertical or horizontal axis, transforming roofs and façades from light to dark, opaque to transparent. Others are rediscovering the use of deciduous vines that grow directly on a building, adding color to a pallet of seasonal changes. Still, such important explorations often seem to involve freestanding buildings either in cities or in rural locations, not buildings that need to relate closely to their neighbors.

A dynamic interpretation of the solar envelope will expand possibilities in dense urban settings. And while the map only shows cities of 5 million or more, many smaller cities around the world can also benefit from solar-envelope zoning and the use of the interstitium.

Frameworks for building have always been as important as the buildings themselves. Besides the aforementioned examples of Acoma in New Mexico and Rajasthan in northwestern India, a case in point is the layout of Olynthus, a colonial town in ancient Greece. At a time of unprecedented expansion of settlements along the Mediterranean shores, Greek planners made orderly arrangements that not only allowed for rapid development but that also took best advantage of the sun. Streets that ran long in the east–west direction framed blocks of 10 houses, 5 on each side of the street. As with Acoma and Rajasthan, the framework was spatial, not simply planar. With building heights controlled, the sun could reach into the south-facing courtyards of many different shapes and sizes.

Olynthus, Ancient Greece: Typical 10-house-block layout, each house centered by a south-facing courtyard. (Based on a drawing by J. Walter Graham from plans by Donald N. Wilber in *Excavations at Olynthus: the Hellenic House* by David M. Robinson and J. Walter Graham.)

The interstitium of the solar envelope adds measures of time to the spatial dimensions of such older frameworks. It offers a dynamic reference in which buildings may change: growing, decaying, moving, or disassembling with the seasons. Designers and dwellers alike thus have the opportunity to explore new possibilities for self-expression that derive from the rhythms of a place.

With boundaries that pulse, urban designers may conceive a kinetic landscape. In winter, the lowest envelopes outline a compact and undulating landscape. Spring and fall bring an additional layer of architectural space. Finally, summer adds a third layer of space into which sheltering systems can expand to complete a yearly cycle for seasonal programming and for climate control. The effect is a collective rising and falling of the scene—like breathing.

Overlapping Seasonal Envelopes: The lowest envelope (left), representing winter, is usually employed by municipalities to guarantee year-round solar access, but the interstitial space between the winter and summer envelopes allows buildings to transform with the seasons.

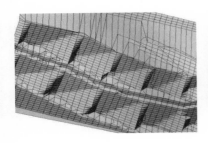
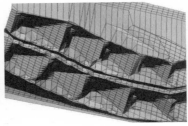

10 | The New Architecture of the Sun

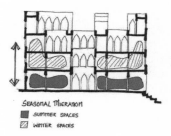

SEASONAL MIGRATION
■ SUMMER SPACES
▨ WINTER SPACES

With assured solar access, we have before us the promise of a new architecture, one that responds to the rhythms of nature. This new architecture of the sun will link us to our own places. It will provide individual choices for comfort. And it will promote the ritual use of space to celebrate our choices.

The basis for this new architecture is the way buildings use energy. Writing on the global impact of increasing energy demands and greenhouse gas emissions, architect Edward Mazria has pointed out that, because most structures are designed to override nature, they presently use 76 percent of all electricity produced in the United States to operate; otherwise, many become uninhabitable—too hot, too cold, no light. Standards and incentives to increase energy efficiency have already been enacted and are unlikely to improve the picture much further. He concludes that achieving further energy efficiency in buildings will require nothing short of a revolution in the design community.[1]

A revolution in the way buildings use energy must involve design education. In referring to a basic lack in his own education, professor of urbanism Witold Rybczynski has complained that the subject of *comfort* was mentioned only once during his entire architectural education, and by a mechanical engineer. "He described something called the 'comfort zone,' which, as far as I can remember, was a kidney-shaped, cross-hatched area on a graph that showed the relationship between temperature and humidity. Comfort was inside the kidney, discomfort was everywhere else. This, apparently, was all that we needed to know about the subject."[2]

Our reliance on mechanical–electrical systems to provide standardized levels of comfort has been linked to Modernism and the celebration of the machine. Yet, even with pronouncements of

Modernism's death after the first energy crisis of the 1970s and the start of the ecology movement, subsequent stylistic movements have shown little recognition of nature, preferring instead to link with critical theory in Poststructuralism. Nor have they had the century-long influence of Modernism with its focus on the important worldwide issue of mechanization. In making a strong case for sustainable architecture, Professor James Steele has written that following Modernism was a 25-year run of Postmodernism, to be replaced in turn by Deconstructivism. Hyped in their turn as the styles of the moment, "the half-lives of subsequent movements seem to have diminished radically."[3]

Yet there are important exceptions to the general indifference of the design community to designing with nature. There are some good examples of solar design in the United States but most have been single buildings, not whole communities. Timothy Beatley, professor of urban and environmental planning, has explained that planners and local officials in the United States can learn from the sustainable-cities movement in Europe where technical and public policy innovations promoting solar design have been adopted. He points out that solar has gained considerable ground there, especially in Germany, the Netherlands, and the Scandinavian countries. Solar is now commonly incorporated into new construction and redevelopment projects. "Several cities . . . are even beginning to describe themselves as 'solar cities,' most notably Frieberg, Berlin, and Saarbruken in Germany."[4]

There are important lessons to be drawn from Beatley's descriptions of solar-design gains in Europe. The first is that the cities he mentions are all in latitudes around 50°N, a highly significant fact proving that nearly all of the world's cities can use solar energy. And the second lesson is that compact urban form and other sustainable design measures need not conflict with a high quality of life. Indeed, just the opposite. "Compact, denser, walkable communities offer tremendous amenities, social and environmental, and are life-enhancing as well as ecologically restorative."[5]

Besides offering the potential to resolve worldwide energy problems, the new architecture must offer variety and choice for those who spend time in a place. Students in my design studio brought this basic fact home to me a few years ago. One spring afternoon, they complained about not being able to relieve conditions in the studio simply by opening a window to the pleasantly cool outside breeze. Since the subject of the studio was designing with nature, I had much sympathy with their frustration in a totally sealed, uniformly conditioned building. When the class met again, the studio was notably more pleasant. The students had unscrewed and set aside the obscure panels below the windows, admitting the most wonderfully refreshing breeze. After some discussion of the matter, we agreed that the panels would surreptitiously stay open for the few remaining weeks of the spring semester. But then they would be quietly replaced for the next class to figure out its own choices for comfort.

People really do need to experience diversity and change, not monotone and universal homogeneity. It is certainly true that there is no pleasure in being uncomfortable. But our systems do not need to deny any variation that might call us to make choices, to give us individual control. Architect Louis Kahn anticipated the potential of variety and choice when he said of his design for the Exeter Library, "You get a book and move toward the light." With that simple declaration, he made a design connection between the dynamism of space, nature, and our participation in it.

The new architecture of the sun will integrate sophisticated mechanical–electrical systems with the more traditional means of migration, transformation, and metabolism. In a more balanced approach to environmental regulation, there is what architect Lisa Heschong has described as the potential for "sensuality, cultural roles, and symbolism that need not, indeed should not, be designed out of existence in the name of a thermally neutral world."[6]

Finally, the new architecture will create the potential for a rich ceremonial life. To fulfill this promise of participation, to enrich life for those who spend time in a place, architecture must ask certain basic questions. Does this place look as though people occupy it? Where is it? What is its rhythm? What is its life? If we cannot answer these questions, we need to think again about our strategies for policy and design.

Notes

CHAPTER 1

1. Gregory Bateson, *Mind and Nature: A Necessary Unity* (New York: E. P. Dutton, 1979), 29, 68.

2. It is ironic that Thomas Edison, developer of the first electrical distribution system, unsuccessfully advocated local grids and local power plants rather than huge, far-flung systems.

3. Ralph Knowles, "For Those Who Spend Time in a Place," *PLACES* 8(2) (1992): 11–14.

CHAPTER 2

1. Ralph L. Knowles, *Energy and Form: An Ecological Approach to Urban Growth* (Cambridge: MIT Press, 1974), 10ff.

2. W. A. Chalfant, *The Story of Inyo* (Stanford: Stanford University Press, 1933).

3. Dora Crouch and June G. Johnson, *Traditions in Architecture: Africa, America, Asia, and Oceania* (New York: Oxford University Press, 2001), 62.

4. Ibid, 63.

5. Labelle Prussin, *African Nomadic Architecture: Space, Place and Gender* (Washington: Smithsonian Institution Press, 1995), 24.

6. Ibid, 23.

7. Dora Crouch and June G. Johnson, *Traditions in Architecture: Africa, America, Asia, and Oceania* (New York: Oxford University Press, 2001), 63.

8. Ibid, 64.

9. Frank Viviano, "Kingdom on Edge: Saudi Arabia." *National Geographic,* October 2003, 19.

10. Lisa Heschong, *Thermal Delight in Architecture* (Cambridge: MIT Press, 1979), 6.

11. John Warren and Ihsan Fethi, *Traditional Houses in Baghdad* (Horsham, England: Coach Publishing House, 1982), 105.

12. G. H. R. Tillotson, ed., *Paradigms of Indian Architecture: Space and Time in Representation and Design* (Richmond, Surrey, Great Britain: Curzon Press, 1998), 166ff.

13. Labelle Prussin, "Shelter for the Soul," in *Shelter: Models of Native Ingenuity,* ed. James Marston Fitch (New York: The Katonah Gallery, 1982), 35.

CHAPTER 3

1. Mary Mix Foley, "The Well-Adjusted House," in *Shelter: Models of Native Ingenuity,* ed. James Marston Fitch (New York: The Katonah Gallery, 1982), 27–34.

2. Ibid.

3. Susan Ubbelohde, "Oak Alley: The Heavy Mass Plantation House," *Proceedings: Eleventh National Passive Conference* (Boulder, CO: American Solar Energy Society, 1986): 358–363.

4. Chris Hellier, *Splendors of Istanbul: Houses and Palaces along the Bosphorus* (New York: Abbeville Press Publishers, 1993), 122.

5. Torvald Faegre, *Tents: Architecture of the Nomads* (Garden City, NY: Anchor Press/Doubleday, 1979).

6. John S. Reynolds, *Courtyards: Aesthetic, Social, and Thermal Delight* (New York: John Wiley & Sons, 2002).

7. Ibid., 143–153.

8. Ralph L. Knowles and Kavita Rodrigues, "The Traditional Indian House: Its Rhythms and Rituals." *Solar 2004: A Solar Harvest: Growing Opportunities: Proceedings of 33d ASES Annual Conference and of 29th National Passive Solar Conference* (Boulder, CO: American Solar Energy Society, 2004): 733–737.

9. V. S. Pramer, *Haveli: Wooden Houses and Mansions of Gujarat* (Ahmedabad, India: Mapin Publishing Pvt. Ltd., 1989), 153ff.

10. Yukio Futagawa and Teiji Itoh, *The Essential Japanese House: Craftsmanship, Function, and Style in Town and Country* (New York: Harper & Row, 1967), 13–15.

11. Ibid., 14.

12. Ibid.

13. Ibid.

CHAPTER 4

1. Barbara Tuchman, *A Distant Mirror* (New York: Knopf, 1979), 11.

2. Robert Brucemann and Donald Prowler, "19th Century Mechanical Systems," *Journal of Architectural Education*, February (1977): 11–15.

3. Henry-Russell Hitchcock, *The Architecture of H. H. Richardson and His Times* (Cambridge, MA: MIT Press, 1966), 106.

CHAPTER 5

1. Daniel Mac-Hir Hutton, *Old Shakertown and the Shakers*, rev. 14th ed. (Harrodsburg, KY: Harrodsburg Herald Press, 1987).

2. Justin McCann, trans., *The Rule of Saint Benedict* (London: Sheed & Ward, 1970), ch. 15.

3. Eviatar Zerubavel, *Hidden Rhythms: Schedules and Calendars in Social Life* (Chicago: University of Chicago Press, 1981), 36f.

4. Umberto Eco, *Art and Beauty in the Middle Ages*, trans. Hugh Bredin (New Haven: Yale University Press, 1986), 44.

5. Ralph L. Knowles, "Rhythm and Ritual: A Motive for Design," in *Proceedings: ACSA Western Regional Meeting*, Paper Session 3A ed. J. Noe and G. Tyau. (Honolulu: University of Hawaii at Manoa, 1996).

6. Eviatar Zerubavel, *Hidden Rhythms: Schedules and Calendars in Social Life* (Chicago: University of Chicago Press, 1981), Chapter 1; Lewis Mumford, *Technics and Civilization* (New York: Harbinger, 1963), 16.

7. Mary Douglas, *Natural Symbols: Explorations in Cosmology* (London: Barrie and Jenkins Ltd., 1978), 19.

8. Carol Venolia, "Design for Life: For Every Season," *Natural Home*, May/June 2003, 40f.

9. Erla Zwingle, "Cities," *National Geographic*, November 2002, 76–78.

CHAPTER 6

1. Timothy Beatley, *Native to Nowhere: Sustaining Home and Community in a Global Age* (Washington, DC: Island Press, 2004), 12.

2. Thomas Hardy, *The Mayor of Casterbridge* (New York: Modern Library, 2002).

3. Langdon C. White, Edwin J. Foscue, and Tom L. McKnight, eds,

Regional Geography of Anglo-America, 4th ed. (Englewood Cliffs, NJ: Prentice-Hall, 1974), 17.

4. Ibid., 299.

5. The US Land Ordinance of 1785 did not come into actual application until 1875 in northwestern Ohio. These earlier surveys in Ashtabula County in northeastern Ohio followed its general principles but with dimensional variations such as a 25-square-mile township instead of the later 36 square miles that partitioned the western lands to the Pacific Ocean.

6. William Williams, *History of Ashtabula County, Ohio, 1798–1878* (Philadelphia: Williams Bros, 1878).

7. Moina Large, *History of Ashtabula County, Ohio*, vol. 1 (Topeka-Indianapolis: Historical Publishing Co., 1924), 403.

8. William Williams, *History of Ashtabula County, Ohio, 1798–1878* (Philadelphia: Williams Bros, 1878).

9. Langdon C. White, Edwin J. Foscue, and Tom L. McKnight, eds, *Regional Geography of Anglo-America*, 4th ed. (Englewood Cliffs, NJ: Prentice-Hall, 1974), 294.

10. William Williams, *History of Ashtabula County, Ohio, 1798–1878* (Philadelphia: Williams Bros, 1878), 134.

11. Ibid, 131.

12. Ibid, 130.

13. Ibid, 135.

14. Langdon C. White, Edwin J. Foscue, and Tom L. McKnight, eds, *Regional Geography of Anglo-America*, 4th ed. (Englewood Cliffs, NJ: Prentice-Hall, 1974), 58.

CHAPTER 7

1. Jeffrey Eugenides, *Middlesex* (New York: Farrar, Straus and Giroux, 2002), 95.

2. Ibid.

3. Caitlin Liu, "Southland's Population Still on the Rise," *Los Angeles Times*, February 14, 2004, B6.

4. NASA Study, "IN BRIEF: Most Fertile Soil in U.S. is Covered by Cities," *Los Angeles Times*, February 14, 2004, A14.

5. United States Census Bureau, "Global Population at a Glance: 2002 and Beyond: International Brief," US Dept. of Commerce, Economics and Statistics Administration, March 2004. http://www.census.gov/ipc/prod/wp02/wp02-1.pdf.

6. Lou Dobbs, "The Dobbs Report: Dangerously Dependent," *U.S. News & World Report*, February 2004, 40.

7. Erla Zwingle, "Cities," *National Geographic*, November 2002, 70–99.

8. Ibid., 85.

9. Ibid., 78.

10. Ralph L. Knowles and Richard D. Berry, *Solar Envelope Concepts: Moderate Density Building Applications*, SERI/SP-98155-1, UC Category: UC-58a, 58b, 58d (Springfield, VA: National Technical Information Service, US Dept. of Commerce, 1980).

11. David Goodstein, "Opinion: Beyond Fossilized Thinking, " *Los Angeles Times*, February 15, 2004.

CHAPTER 8

1. Fredrick R. Steiner, *The Living Landscape: An Ecological Approach to Landscape Planning* (New York: McGraw-Hill, 1991), x.

2. Ralph L. Knowles, *Energy and Form: An Ecological Approach to Urban Growth* (Cambridge, MA: MIT Press, 1974), 27–33; and Ralph L. Knowles, *Sun Rhythm Form* (Cambridge, MA: MIT Press, 1981), 143–144.

3. Ralph L. Knowles, "The Solar Envelope," *Solar Law Reporter*, 2 (July/August 1980): 263–297.

4. Ralph L. Knowles, *Sun Rhythm Form* (Cambridge, MA: MIT Press, 1981), 121–125.

5. Ralph L. Knowles, "Solar Access and Urban Form," *AIA Journal* (February 1980): 42ff; and Ralph L. Knowles, *Sun Rhythm Form* (Cambridge, MA: MIT Press, 1981), 39.

6. Kevin Lynch, *The Image of the City* (Cambridge, MA: The Technology Press & Harvard University Press, 1960), 3.

7. Ralph L. Knowles, "The Solar Envelope," in *Time-Saver Standards for Urban Design*, eds. D. Watson, A. Plattus, and R. Shibley (New York: McGraw-Hill, 2003): 4.6-1ff.

CHAPTER 9

1. Eduardo Catalano, *Floralis Generica* (Cambridge, MA: Cambridge Architectural Press, 2002), 2.

2. Ralph L. Knowles and Karen M. Kensek, "The Interstitium: A Zoning Strategy for Seasonally Adaptive Architecture" in *Proceedings of PLEA 2000: Architecture, City, Environment*, eds. K. Steemers and S. Yannas (London: James & James Ltd, 2000), 773f.

3. John S. Reynolds, *Courtyards: Aesthetic, Social, and Thermal Delight* (New York: John Wiley & Sons, 2002), 3.

4. Ibid., 148.

5. A separate bibliography is provided specifically containing recent books on climate-adaptive architecture.

CHAPTER 10

1. Edward Mazria, "It's the Architecture, Stupid!" *Solar Today*, May/June 2003, 48ff.

2. Witold Rybczynski, *Home: A Short History of an Idea* (New York: Penguin, 1987), vii.

3. James Steele, *Sustainable Architecture: Principles, Paradigms, and Case Studies* (New York: McGraw-Hill, 1997), 229.

4. Timothy Beatley, *Green Urbanism: Learning from European Cities* (Washington, DC: Island Press, 2000), 270.

5. Ibid., 415.

6. Lisa Heschong, *Thermal Delight in Architecture* (Cambridge, MA: MIT Press, 1979), 17.

Bibliography

Atlas of Ashtabula Co., Ohio. 1874. Philadelphia: Titus, Simmons and Titus.

Bateson, Gregory. 1979. *Mind and Nature: A Necessary Unity.* New York: E. P. Dutton.

Beatley, Timothy. 2000. *Green Urbanism: Learning from European Cities.* Washington, DC: Island Press.

——2004. *Native to Nowhere: Sustaining Home and Community in a Global Age.* Washington, DC: Island Press.

Beatley, Timothy and Kristy Manning. 1997. *The Ecology of Place: Planning for Environment, Economy, and Community.* Washington, DC: Island Press.

Benfield, F. Kaid, et al. 2000. *Solving Sprawl: Models of Smart Growth in Communities across America.* Washington, DC: Natural Resources Council; Dist. by Island Press.

Breen, Ann and Dick Rigby. 2005. *Intown Living: A Different American Dream.* Washington, DC: Island Press.

Brucemann, Robert and Donald Prowler. 1977. "19th Century Mechanical Systems," *Journal of Architectural Education,* February: 11–15.

Bullard, Robert, Glenn S. Johnson, and Angel O. Torres. 2000. *Sprawl City: Race, Politics, and Planning in Atlanta.* Washington, DC: Island Press.

Burchell, Robert, et al. 2005. *Sprawl Costs: Economic Impacts of Unchecked Development.* Washington, DC: Island Press.

Calthorpe, Peter and William Fulton. 2001. *The Regional City: Planning for the End of Sprawl.* Washington, DC: Island Press.

Catalano, Eduardo. 2002. *Floralis Generica*. Cambridge, MA: Cambridge Architectural Press.

Chalfant, W. A. 1933. *The Story of Inyo*. Stanford, CA: Stanford University Press.

Crouch, Dora P. and June G. Johnson. 2001. *Traditions in Architecture: Africa, America, Asia, and Oceania*. New York: Oxford University Press.

Crump, Ralph W. and Martin J. Harms, eds. 1981. *The Design Connection: Energy and Technology in Architecture*. Preston Thomas Memorial Series in Architecture. New York: Van Nostrand Reinhold Co.

Dobbs, Lou. 2004. "The Dobbs Report: Dangerously dependent," *U.S. News & World Report,* February: 40.

Douglas, Mary. 1978. *Natural Symbols: Explorations in Cosmology*. London: Barrie and Jenkins Ltd.

Duerksen, Chris and Cara Snyder. 2005. *Nature-Friendly Communities*. Washington, DC: Island Press.

Eco, Umberto. 1986. *Art and Beauty in the Middle Ages*. Trans. Hugh Bredin. New Haven, CT: Yale University Press.

Eugenides, Jeffrey. 2002. *Middlesex*. New York: Farrar, Straus and Giroux.

Faegre, Torvald. 1979. *Tents: Architecture of the Nomads*. Garden City, NY: Anchor Press/Doubleday.

Faragher, John Mack. 1986. *Sugar Creek: Life on the Illinois Prairie*. New Haven, CT: Yale University Press.

Filippidis, Dimitris, ed. 1990. *Greek Traditional Architecture: Peloponnese*. Athens: Melissa.

Foley, Mary Mix. 1982. "The Well-Adjusted House." In James Marston Fitch, ed., *Shelter: Models of Native Ingenuity*. New York: The Katonah Gallery.

Freese, Barbara. 2004. *Coal: A Human History*. London: Penguin Books Ltd.

Frumkin, Howard, et al. 2004. *Urban Sprawl and Public Health: Designing, Planning, and Building for Healthy Communities*. Washington, DC: Island Press.

Futagawa, Yukio and Teiji Itoh. 1967. *The Essential Japanese House: Craftsmanship, Function, and Style in Town and Country*. Jointly published by New York: Harper & Row and Tokyo: John Weatherhill.

Gillham, Oliver. 2002. *The Limitless City: A Primer on the Urban Sprawl Debate*. Washington, DC: Island Press.

Goodstein, David, 2004. "Opinion: Beyond Fossilized Thinking." *Los Angeles Times,* 15 February.

Hardy, Thomas. 2002. *The Mayor of Casterbridge.* New York: Modern Library.

Hayes, Gail Boyer. 1979. *Solar Access Law.* Cambridge, MA: Ballinger.

Heilbron, J. L. 1999. *The Sun in the Church: Cathedrals as Solar Observatories.* Cambridge and London: Harvard University Press.

Hellier, Chris. 1993. *Splendors of Istanbul: Houses and Palaces along the Bosphorus.* New York and London: Abbeville Press.

Heschong, Lisa. 1979. *Thermal Delight in Architecture.* Cambridge, MA: MIT Press.

Hiss, Tony. 1990. *The Experience of Place.* New York: Knopf.

Hitchcock, Henry-Russell. 1966. *The Architecture of H. H. Richardson and His Times.* Cambridge, MA: MIT Press.

Hough, Michael. 1984. *City Form and Natural Process: Towards a New Urban Vernacular.* London: Croom Helm.

Hutton, Daniel Mac-Hir. 1987. *Old Shakertown and the Shakers.* Rev. 14th ed. Harrodsburg, KY: Harrodsburg Herald Press.

Knowles, Ralph L. 1974. *Energy and Form: An Ecological Approach to Urban Growth.* Cambridge, MA: MIT Press.

—— 1980a. "Solar Access and Urban Form." *AIA Journal,* February: 42ff.

—— 1980b. "The Solar Envelope," *Solar Law Reporter,* 2 (July/August): 263–297.

—— 1981. *Sun Rhythm Form.* Cambridge, MA: MIT Press.

—— 1992. "For Those Who Spend Time in a Place," *PLACES* 8(2)(Fall): 11–14.

—— 1996. "Rhythm and Ritual: A Motive for Design," Paper Session 3A. In J. Noe and G. Tyau, eds., *Proceedings: ACSA Western Regional Meeting.* Honolulu: University of Hawaii at Manoa.

—— 2003. "The Solar Envelope." In D. Watson, A. Plattus, and R. Shibley, eds., *Time-Saver Standards for Urban Design.* New York: McGraw-Hill: 4.6-1–4.6-18.

—— 2005a. "The Growing Need for Solar-Access Zoning." Technical Session: Sustainable Urban Planning. In D.Y. Goswami, S. Vijayaraghaven, and R. Campbell-Howe, eds., *Proceedings of the 2005 Solar World Congress.* (Combined Proceedings of ISES, ASES 34th Annual Conference, and 30th National Passive Solar Conference. Orlando, FL.

—— 2005b. "The Interstitium and the Ritual Use of Space." Technical

Session: Passive Architecture in Perspective. In D.Y. Goswami, S. Vijayaraghaven, and R. Campbell-Howe, eds., *Proceedings of the 2005 Solar World Congress*. (Combined Proceedings of ISES, ASES 34th Annual Conference, and 30th National Passive Solar Conference. Orlando, FL.

Knowles, Ralph L. and Richard D. Berry. 1980. *Solar Envelope Concepts: Moderate Density Building Applications*. SERI/SP-98155-1, UC Category: UC-58a, 58b, 58d. Springfield, VA: National Technical Information Service, US Dept. of Commerce.

Knowles, Ralph L. and Karen M. Kensek. 2000. "The Interstitium: A zoning strategy for seasonally adaptive architecture." In K. Steemers and S. Yannas, eds., *Proceedings of PLEA 2000: Architecture, City, Environment*. London, UK: James & James Ltd: 773f.

Knowles, Ralph L. and Pierre F. Koenig. 2002. "Dynamic Adaptations for Courtyard Buildings." In R. Campbell-Howe, ed., *Solar 2002: Sunrise on the Reliable Energy Economy: Proceedings of 31st ASES Annual Conference and of 27th National Passive Solar Conference*. Boulder, CO: American Solar Energy Society: 583–589.

Knowles, Ralph L. and Kavita Rodrigues. 2004. "The Traditional Indian House: Its Rhythms and Rituals." *Solar 2004: A Solar Harvest: Growing Opportunities: Proceedings of 33rd ASES Annual Conference and of 29th National Passive Solar Conference*. Boulder, CO: American Solar Energy Society: 733–737.

Knudsen, H.N., et al. 1989. *Thermal Comfort in Passive Solar Buildings: Final Report to the Commission of the European Communities, Directorate-General for Science, Research and Development. Research Project EN3S-0035-DK(B)*. Lyngby Copenhagen: Technical University of Denmark: 117ff.

Large, Moina W. 1924. *History of Ashtabula County, Ohio*. Vol. 1 of 2. Topeka-Indianapolis: Historical Publishing.

Liu, Caitlin. 2004. "Southland's Population Still on the Rise." *Los Angeles Times*, 14 February: B6.

Lyle, John Tillman. 1985. *Design for Human Ecosystems: Landscape, Land Use, and Natural Resources*. New York: Van Nostrand Reinhold.

—— 1994. *Regenerative Design for Sustainable Development*. New York: John Wiley & Sons.

Lynch, Kevin. 1960. *The Image of the City*. Cambridge, MA: The Technology Press & Harvard University Press.

Mazria, Edward. 2003. "It's the Architecture, Stupid!" *Solar Today*, May/June: 48ff.

McCann, Justin, trans. 1970. *The Rule of Saint Benedict*. London: Sheed & Ward.

McHarg, Ian L. 1992. *Design With Nature*. New York: John Wiley & Sons.

Meyer, Marvin and Richard Smith, eds. 1994. *Ancient Christian Magic: Coptic Texts of Ritual Power*. New York: Harper Collins.

Meyerson, Frederick A. B. 2005. *Outgrowing America: Population, Politics, and the 21st Century*. Washington, DC: Smithsonian Books.

—— 2003. "Population, Biodiversity, and Changing Climate." *Advances in Applied Biodiversity Science*, 4(August): 83–90.

Mumford, Lewis. 1963. *Technics and Civilization*. New York: Harbinger.

NASA Study. 2004. "IN BRIEF: Most Fertile Soil in U.S. is Covered by Cities." *Los Angeles Times*, 14 February: A14.

Newman, Peter and Jeffrey Kenworthy. 1999. *Sustainability and Cities: Overcoming Automobile Dependence*. Washington, DC: Island Press.

Olgyay, Aladar. 1957. *Solar Control and Shading Devices [by] Olgyay and Olgyay*. New Jersey: Princeton University Press.

Oliver, Paul, ed. 1997. *Encyclopedia of the Vernacular Architecture of the World*. Cambridge, UK: Cambridge University Press.

Platt, Rutherford H. 2004. *Land Use and Society: Geography, Law, and Public Policy*. rev. ed. Washington, DC: Island Press.

Pramer, V.S. 1989. *Haveli: Wooden Houses and Mansions of Gujarat*. Ahmedabad, India: Mapin Publishing Pvt. Ltd.

Prigogine, Ilya and Isabelle Stengers. 1984. *Order Out of Chaos*. Toronto: Bantam Books.

Prussin, Labelle. 1982. "Shelter for the Soul." In James Marston Fitch, ed., *Shelter: Models of Native Ingenuity*. New York: The Katonah Gallery, 35–42.

—— 1995. *African Nomadic Architecture: Space, Place and Gender*. Washington: Smithsonian Institution Press.

Putnam, Robert D. 2000. *Bowling Alone: the Collapse and Revival of American Community*. New York: Simon & Schuster.

Randolph, John. 2004. *Environmental Land Use Planning and Management*. Washington, DC: Island Press.

Rapaport, Amos. 1969. *House Form and Culture*. Englewood Cliffs, NJ: Prentice-Hall.

Ravereau, Andre. 1989. *La Casbah d'Alger*. Paris: Editions Sindbad.

Reynolds, John S. 2002. *Courtyards: Aesthethic, Social, and Thermal Delight*. New York: John Wiley & Sons.

Robinson, David M. and J. Walter Graham. 1938. *Excavations at Olynthus: The Hellenic House*. Baltimore: Johns Hopkins University Press.

Rotella, Sebastian. 2004. "Kadafi Pitches His Tent in Brussels." *Los Angeles Times*, 28 April: A1.

Rybczynski, Witold. 1987. *Home: A Short History of an Idea*. New York: Penguin Group (USA).

Solomon, Daniel. 2003. *Global City Blues*. Washington, DC: Island Press.

Spirn, Anne Whiston. 1984. *The Granite Garden: Urban Nature and Human Design*. New York: Basic Books.

Steele, James. 1997. *Sustainable Architecture: Principles, Paradigms, and Case Studies*. New York: McGraw-Hill.

Steemers, Koen and Mary Ann Steane, eds. 2004. *Environmental Diversity in Architecture*. London: Spon Press/Taylor & Francis Group.

Steiner, Frederick R. 2002. *Human Ecology: Following Nature's Lead*. Washington, DC: Island Press.

—— 1991. *The Living Landscape: An Ecological Approach to Landscape Planning*. New York: McGraw-Hill.

Thompson, George F. and Frederick R. Steiner, eds. 1997. *Ecological Design and Planning*. New York: John Wiley & Sons.

Thompson, J. William and Kim Sorvig. 2000. *Sustainable Landscape Construction: A Guide to Green Building Outdoors*. Washington, DC: Island Press.

Thrower, Norman J. W. 1966. *Original Survey and Land Subdivision: A Comparative Study of the Form and Effect of Contrasting Cadastral Surveys*. The Monograph Series of the Association of American Geographers, vol. 4. Chicago: Rand McNally & Co.

Tillotson, G. H. R., ed. 1998. *Paradigms of Indian Architecture: Space and Time in Representation and Design*. Richmond, Surrey, Great Britain: Curzon Press.

Todd, Nancy Jack. 2005. *A Safe and Sustainable World*. Washington, DC: Island Press.

Tuchman, Barbara W. 1979. *A Distant Mirror*. New York: Knopf.

Ubbelohde, M. Susan. 1986. "Oak Alley: The Heavy Mass Plantation House." *Proceedings: Eleventh National Passive Conference*. Boulder, CO: American Solar Energy Society: 358–363.

United Nations, Dept. of Economic and Social Affairs: Population Division. *Urban Agglomerations 2003*. www.un.org/esa/population/publications/wup2003/2003UrbanAgglomeration2003-Web.xls.

United States Census Bureau. Global Population at a Glance: 2002 and Beyond: International Brief. March 2004. US Dept. of Commerce, Economics and Statistics Administration: WP/02-1. www.census.gov/ipc/www/world.html.

Van der Ryn, Sim and Peter Calthorpe, eds. 1991. *Sustainable Communities: A New Design Synthesis for Cities, Suburbs, and Towns*. San Francisco: Sierra Club Books.

Venolia, Carol. 2003. "Design for Life: For Every Season." *Natural Home*, May/June: 40f.

Viviano, Frank. 2003. "Kingdom on Edge: Saudi Arabia." *National Geographic*, October: 2–41.

Ward, Barbara. 1976. *The Home of Man*. New York: W. W. Norton & Company.

Warren, John and Ihsan Fethi. 1982. *Traditional Houses in Baghdad*. Horsham, England: Coach Publishing House.

Watson, Donald. 1977. *Designing and Building a Solar House: Your Place in the Sun*. Charlotte, VT: Garden Way Publishing.

—— ed. 1979. *Energy Conservation through Building Design*. New York: McGraw-Hill.

Watson, Donald and Kenneth Labs. 1983. *Climatic Design: Energy-Efficient Building Principles and Practices*. New York: McGraw-Hill.

Watson, Donald, et al., eds. 2003. *Time-Saver Standards for Urban Design*. New York: McGraw-Hill.

White, C. Langdon, Edwin J. Foscue, and Tom L. McKnight, eds. 1974. *Regional Geography of Anglo-America*. 4th ed. Englewood Cliffs, NJ: Prentice-Hall.

Williams, William W. 1878. *History of Ashtabula County, Ohio, 1798–1878*. Philadelphia: Williams Bros.

Zerubavel, Eviatar. 1981. *Hidden Rhythms: Schedules and Calendars in Social Life*. Chicago: University of Chicago Press.

Zwingle, Erla. 2002. "Cities." *National Geographic*, November: 70–99.

FOR ADDITIONAL READING

Some recent books on dynamic architectural adaptations to climate, not referenced in text:

Gausa, Manuel and Jaime Salazar. 2002. *Single-Family Housing*. Barcelona: Actar Publishers and Basel: Birkhauser.

Gissen, David, ed. 2002. *Big and Green: Towards Sustainable Architecture in the 21st Century*. New York: Princeton Architectural Press.

Guzowski, Mary. 2000. *Daylighting for Sustainable Design*. New York: McGraw-Hill.

Hawkes, Dean and Wayne Forster. 2002. *Energy Efficient Buildings: Architecture, Engineering, and Environment*. New York: W. W. Norton & Company.

Hezog, Thomas, ed. 1996. *Solar Energy in Architecture and Urban Planning*. New York: Prestel.

Ho, Cathy Lang and Raul A. Barreneche. 2001. *House: American Houses for the New Century*. New York: Universe Publishing.

Jones, David Lloyd. 1998. *Architecture and the Environment: Bioclimatic Building Design*. Woodstock, NY: The Overlook Press, Peter Mayer Publishers.

Mollerup, Per. 2001. *Collapsible*. San Francisco, CA: Chronicle Books.

Mostaedi, Arian. 2002. *Sustainable Architecture: Low Tech Houses*. Barcelona: Carles Broto & Josep Ma Minguet.

Ngo, Dung. 2003. *World House Now*. New York: Universe Publishing.

Pople, Nicolas. 2003. *Small Houses*. New York: Universe Publishing.

Riewoldt, Otto. 1997. *Intelligent Spaces*. London: Laurence King Publishing.

Siegal, Jennifer, ed. 2002. *Mobile: The Art of Portable Architecture*. New York, NY: Princeton Architectural Press.

Slessor, Catherine. 1997. *Eco-Tech: Sustainable Architecture and High Technology*. New York: Thames & Hudson.

Yeang, Ken. 1999. *The Green Skyscraper: The Basis for Designing Sustainable Intensive Buildings*. Munich: Prestel Verlag.

Wang, Wilfried. 1998. *Herzog & de Meuron*. Basel: Birkhauser Verlag.

Wines, James. 2000. *Green Architecture*. Cologne: Taschen.

Index